# Weiss Ratings' Consumer Guide to Health Savings Accounts

# Weiss Ratings'
# Consumer Guide to
# Health Savings Accounts

**Spring 2013**

**GREY HOUSE PUBLISHING**

Weiss Ratings
15430 Endeavour Drive
Jupiter, FL 33478
561-627-3300

Published by Grey House Publishing, Inc. located at 4919 Route 22, Amenia, NY, 12501; telephone 518-789-8700. Grey House Publishing neither guarantees the accuracy of the data contained herein nor assumes any responsibility for errors, omissions or discrepancies. Grey House Publishing accepts no payment for listing; inclusion in the publication of any organization, agency, institution, publication, service or individual does not imply endorsement of the publisher.

4919 Route 22
PO Box 56
Amenia, NY 12501-0056

Spring 2013 Edition

ISBN: 978-1-61925-047-5
ISSN: 2164-4195

# CONTENTS

# Terms and Conditions

This Document is prepared strictly for the confidential use of our customer(s). It has been provided to you at your specific request. It is not directed to, or intended for distribution to or use by, any person or entity who is a citizen or resident of or located in any locality, state, country or other jurisdiction where such distribution, publication, availability or use would be contrary to law or regulation or which would subject Weiss Ratings or its affiliates to any registration or licensing requirement within such jurisdiction.

No part of the analysts' compensation was, is, or will be, directly or indirectly, related to the specific recommendations or views expressed in this research report.

This Document is not intended for the direct or indirect solicitation of business. Weiss Ratings, LLC and its affiliates disclaim any and all liability to any person or entity for any loss or damage caused, in whole or in part, by any error (negligent or otherwise) or other circumstances involved in, resulting from or relating to the procurement, compilation, analysis, interpretation, editing, transcribing, publishing and/or dissemination or transmittal of any information contained herein.

Weiss Ratings has not taken any steps to ensure that the securities or investment vehicle referred to in this report are suitable for any particular investor. The investment or services contained or referred to in this report may not be suitable for you and it is recommended that you consult an independent investment advisor if you are in doubt about such investments or investment services. Nothing in this report constitutes investment, legal, accounting or tax advice or a representation that any investment or strategy is suitable or appropriate to your individual circumstances or otherwise constitutes a personal recommendation to you.

The ratings and other opinions contained in this Document must be construed solely as statements of opinion from Weiss Ratings, Inc., and not statements of fact. Each rating or opinion must be weighed solely as a factor in your choice of an institution and should not be construed as a recommendation to buy, sell or otherwise act with respect to the particular product or company involved.

Past performance should not be taken as an indication or guarantee of future performance, and no representation or warranty, expressed or implied, is made regarding future performance. Information, opinions and estimates contained in this report reflect a judgment at its original date of publication and are subject to change without notice. Weiss Ratings offers a notification service for rating changes on companies you specify. For more information call 1-877-934-7778 or visit www.weissratings.com. The price, value and income from any of the securities or financial instruments mentioned in this report can fall as well as rise.

This Document and the information contained herein is copyrighted by Weiss Ratings, LLC Any copying, displaying, selling, distributing or otherwise delivering of this information or any part of this Document to any other person, without the express written consent of Weiss Ratings, LLC except by a reviewer or editor who may quote brief passages in connection with a review or a news story, is prohibited.

---

### Weiss Ratings' Mission Statement

Weiss Ratings' mission is to empower consumers, professionals, and institutions with high quality advisory information for selecting or monitoring a financial services company or financial investment. In doing so, Weiss Ratings will adhere to the highest ethical standards by maintaining our independent, unbiased outlook and approach to advising our customers.

# Part I:

# The Basics of Health Savings Accounts

## About This Guide

Americans are worried about soaring health care costs and access to affordable care. In response to those concerns, in March 2010, President Obama signed into law the *Patient Protection and Affordable Care Act* and the *Health Care and Education Reconciliation Act of 2010*. The intentions of the acts include expanding health coverage, protecting existing coverage, and reducing costs. However, it will take many years to measure the effects of all of the new laws' measures.

That means it's up to you to explore ways to keep your health care costs down. And in this guide, we show you one way to get more control over your spending by using a Health Savings Account (HSA). Signed into law by President George W. Bush, as part of the *Medicare Prescription Drug, Improvement, and Modernization Act of 2003*, an HSA is an alternative to traditional health insurance that will let you pay for current health expenses and save for future ones on a tax-free basis.

Although an HSA is not for everyone, it could be worthwhile if any of the following applies to you:

- You are healthy and spend little on medical care,

- You have a controlled chronic illness but are otherwise healthy,

- Or you estimate that your savings on health care expenses, together with the tax benefits, outweigh your higher deductible.

## How Health Savings Accounts Work

An HSA is an account into which you or your employer deposit money to be used solely for expenses related to you or your family's health care. The money deposited is not taxed by the IRS and grows tax-free. Withdrawals you take to pay qualified medical expenses are tax-free also. And any money you don't use during the year simply stays in your account for you to use in the future.

In addition to cutting your taxes and reducing your health insurance premiums, you own and control the money in your account. You get to make the spending decisions without having to wait for permission from a third party or a health insurer. You are also responsible for investing the money in your account. Don't worry, though. You can get advice from the HSA trustee or custodian.

There are no minimum or maximum income limits on who may contribute to an HSA, nor do you need to have earned income. Therefore, your HSA contributions can come from your own personal money, dividend income, or unemployment or welfare benefits. But even though there are no income limits that affect HSA eligibility, you still must file a federal income tax return to ensure that you receive all the tax benefits HSAs offer.

Before you can open an HSA, however, you must have a …

## High-Deductible Health Plan (HDHP)

An eligible high-deductible health plan (HDHP) is insurance that does not cover first-dollar medical expenses but rather is designed to cover catastrophic medical expenses. It may, however, have limited exceptions for dental, vision, and preventive care first-dollar coverage. It can be an HMO, a PPO, or an indemnity plan as long as it meets the legal requirements.

To qualify as an HDHP in 2013, the plan must include minimum deductibles of $1,250 for individual coverage and $2,500 for family coverage. Annual out-of-pocket expenses, including deductibles and co-pays, cannot exceed $6,250 for individual coverage and $12,500 for family coverage. Both amounts are indexed annually for inflation.

### Annual HDHP Deductibles in 2013

|  | Individual Coverage | Family Coverage |
|---|---|---|
| Minimum | $1,250 | $2,500 |
| Maximum | $6,250 | $12,500 |

---

## "Significant Benefits" Defined

**Although an insurance plan may be designed with reasonable benefit restrictions limiting the plan's covered benefits, it must provide coverage offering significant benefits over and above the restrictions.**

**In addition to covering expenses for hospitalization or inpatient care, a plan must include benefits such as payment for visits to doctors' offices and outpatient care.**

**Additionally, there must be a reasonable limit to payments for out-of-pocket expenses.**

Just because a health plan meets the minimum deductible requirements it's not automatically considered a qualifying HDHP. It must also provide significant benefits. Hence, a limited health plan that provides a fixed amount per day of hospitalization; a fixed amount per office visit with a physician; a fixed amount per out-patient treatment at a hospital; a fixed amount per ambulance use; and coverage for expenses relating to the treatment of a specified list of diseases would not meet the criteria for significant benefits and not qualify as a HDHP.

For example, suppose you're looking at a plan that includes hospital care and medical services, including surgery. But it excludes visits to the hospital emergency room, a trauma center, a doctor's office or a clinic. This plan would not qualify as an HDHP since there is a restriction on benefits to medical

services while the covered individual is admitted to a hospital or at a same-day surgery facility. That is considered unreasonable, because significant other benefits do not remain available under the plan.

Although the high-deductible portion of the insurance could make HDHPs impractical for some people, many others might consider the significant tax benefit extremely valuable. What's more, an HDHP generally costs less than traditional health care coverage, so the money you save on insurance can be put into the HSA where it grows tax-free.

You should be aware, however, that HDHPs can have higher out-of-pocket co-pays and coinsurance for non-network services than traditional insurance. All covered benefits, including prescription drugs, must apply to the plan's annual deductible. If they don't, the plan will not qualify as an HDHP and you won't be eligible for an HSA.

You should be aware, however, that HDHPs can have higher out-of-pocket co-pays and coinsurance for non-network services than traditional insurance. All covered benefits, including prescription drugs, must apply to the plan's annual deductible. If they don't, the plan will not qualify as an HDHP and you won't be eligible for an HSA.

The HDHP policy does not have to be in your name. As long as you have coverage under the HDHP policy, you can be eligible for an HSA assuming you meet the other eligibility requirements.

Spouses will commonly share the same policy. However, there could be times when it might make sense for each to have individual policies, for example when the HDHP is provided through an employer where premiums might be lower.

Finally, be sure to get second and third opinions before you buy an HDHP. Ask competing agents to offer you policies, then carefully read each one and ask questions to clarify anything you don't understand. Take the policies to a neutral third party, such as a financial planner, to get yet another opinion.

# Part II:

# HSA Eligibility, Ownership, and Control

# HSA Eligibility

You are eligible for an HSA if you:

- Are covered by an HDHP,

- Are not covered by other health insurance,

- Are not enrolled in Medicare, and

- Can't be claimed as a dependent on someone else's tax return.

What's more, if you are a single parent with a dependent child or other relative, you can be eligible for an HSA even if your dependent has non-HDHP coverage.

Under Internal Revenue Service (IRS) rules, general health care flexible spending accounts (FSAs) are not available to HSA participants. An FSA is a pre-funded health spending account that employees pay into over the year to help offset medical costs.

Nor can you use a health reimbursement account (HRA). An HRA is a type of health insurance plan that reimburses employees for qualified medical expenses. In this way it's similar to an FSA.

However, the IRS does permit various HSA/FSA/HRA combinations, including:

- Limited purpose FSAs and HRAs. These restrict your reimbursements to limited benefits such as vision, dental, or preventive care.

- Post-deductible FSAs or HRAs. These only provide reimbursement after the minimum annual deductible has been met under the HDHP.

- Retirement HRAs. These provide reimbursement only for retired employees.

- Suspended HRAs. These are when the employee elects to forgo health reimbursement through the HRA for the coverage period.

So you know you need a high-deductible health plan to go with your HSA. Now you want to know what coverage you should expect through the plan and what coverage you cannot receive while remaining eligible for your HSA.

Here is the coverage you are allowed to have and still be eligible for an HSA. You can:

- Take out a separate policy for specific disease or illness, accident, disability, dental care, vision care and long-term care.

- Take part in an employee assistance program, wellness or disease management program. The key is that these programs must not provide significant benefits in the nature of medical care or treatment.

- Buy COBRA continuation coverage

- Maintain health plan coverage while receiving unemployment compensation

- Pay for Medicare and out-of-pocket expenses for Parts A and B

- Own a Medicare HMO

- Have prescription drug coverage

- Pay your share of premiums for employer-based coverage

- Purchase qualified long-term care insurance

- Use a drug discount card

# Establishing an HSA

An HSA is an exempt trust established through a written governing instrument under state law. State trust law therefore determines when an HSA is established. Most state trust laws require that a trust must be funded to be established. Whether the account beneficiary's signature is required to establish the trust also depends on state law.

Once your high-deductible health plan is in effect you can establish your HSA. If your HDHP coverage is effective on the first day of the month, you can immediately set up your HSA. If your HDHP coverage is effective on any day other than the first day of the month, you'll have to wait until the first day of following the month. There is nothing to stop you from completing all the paperwork for your HSA and making a minimum deposit to your account prior to the effective date of your HDHP coverage. This does not mean that you have established your account, because it is not officially established until your HDHP coverage begins. However, completing the paperwork before your coverage begins ensures that your HSA will be established as early as possible. This is especially important if the first of the month occurs on a non-business day when your HDHP coverage becomes effective.

You can sign up for an HSA at banks, credit unions, insurance companies and other companies approved by the IRS. Your employer can also set up a plan for employees. Insured banks and credit unions are automatically qualified to handle HSAs. Any bank, credit union, or any other entity that currently meets the IRS standards for being a trustee or custodian for an IRA, Archer Medical Savings Account, or MSA can be an HSA trustee or custodian. The law also allows insurance companies to be HSA trustees or custodians.

## HSA Ownership and Control

Joint HSAs are not permitted. You own your account even if your employer contributes to it, and you'll make most of the decisions regarding your account including:

- Whether to contribute to it

- How much to use for medical expenses

- For which medical expenses you will use the account

- Whether you will simply save the money in the account

- Who holds the account (e.g., a bank)

- How to invest the funds in the account

Your employer cannot restrict how your HSA funds are used. And your HSA custodian or trustee has very limited control. If you don't like the restrictions placed on the account, you can simply start a new HSA elsewhere.

Likewise, you alone are responsible for deciding whether the money you spend from your HSA is for a qualified medical expense. If it is used for other than qualified medical expenses, the expenditure will be taxed. And if you are not disabled or over age 65, you'll get hit with a 20% tax penalty for 2013

You should, therefore, learn what qualified medical expenses are, and keep your receipts in case you need to defend your expenditures or decisions during an IRS audit. Plus, if you reach your deductible level, you may need to send those receipts to your HDHP insurer.

> **Good to Know**
> Unlike some forms of savings you may **not** borrow against your HSA or pledge the funds in it.

Funds deposited into your HSA remain in your account even if you lose your HDHP coverage. And they will automatically roll over from one year to the next so you can continue to use them for qualified medical expenses. If you've had HDHP coverage for less than a year, the annual maximum contribution is reduced, so you may need to withdraw some of the money to avoid the tax on excess HSA contributions. It is your responsibility to follow this requirement.

Responsibilities of the trustee or custodian are limited, but there are some reporting requirements. The trustee or custodian must report total contributions made to the account during the year and the value of the account at the end of the year. It will also report the total distributions taken during the year. These reports are completed on IRS forms and must be sent to the HSA owner and the IRS. Your HSA trustee or custodian does, however, have some control regarding the account administration. It may set account fees as well as minimum requirements for deposits, balances, distributions, and distribution timing.

## What's the Difference between a Custodian and a Trustee?

The differences between a "custodian" and a "trustee" are minor. A trust is a legal entity under which assets are actually owned and held on behalf of a beneficiary. The trustee has some level of discretionary fiduciary authority over the assets of the fund. The trustee must exercise that authority in the best interests of the beneficiary.

A custodial arrangement, on the other hand, is like a trust, but the custodian simply holds the assets on behalf of the owner of the assets. Other than holding the assets and doing as the owner orders, the custodian has no fiduciary obligations to the owner.

The determination of what constitutes a trust or custodial arrangement is made under state law. Your account trustee/custodian will determine what you need to do, which may include completing and processing appropriate paperwork and making a minimum deposit.

If your bank or credit union doesn't offer HSAs, you cannot act as your own trustee or custodian. You must establish your HSA with an approved institution. Even if there is not a suitable institution near you, you may be able to find a company willing to open an HSA for you.

An HSA can be administered through a debit card that restricts payments and reimbursements to health care providers as long as the funds in the HSA are otherwise readily available. This means you must be able to access the funds through online transfers, withdrawals from automatic teller machines, or check writing. If this is restricted by your employer, they must explain how to access the funds.

Although an HSA is an individual account, you can allow others to withdraw funds from your account. Remember though that disbursements are subject to tax and penalties if they are not used to pay for qualified medical expenses.

Upon your death, if your spouse is the beneficiary, he or she is treated as the owner of your HSA. To the extent your spouse is not the beneficiary the account will no longer be treated as an HSA upon your death. The account will become part of your estate. Remember that a child is not eligible for an HSA; therefore, you should consult with your financial advisor about how you should pass along the assets in your HSA to your child if he or she is your sole beneficiary.

# Part III:

# Contributions and Expenses

# HSA Contributions

You can make the maximum pre-tax contribution to an HSA on the first day it's established. Your contribution is based on your expected coverage on the first day of the last month of your taxable year.

The first thing to consider as soon as you become eligible might be how much to contribute. Contributions for the tax year can be made in one or more payments, at any time before you're required to file your federal income tax return for the prior year. This is usually April 15, and extensions are excluded.

Neither your tax filing status nor the HDHP deductible affects your contribution level.

There are, however, limits to the maximum you can contribute. They depend on whether you have an individual or a family high-deductible health plan.

For 2013, the most you can contribute to an HSA and deduct from your taxes is $3,250 for individual HDHP coverage and $6,450 if you take family coverage. These amounts are indexed annually.

Contributions to an HSA can be made by you, your employer, or both. If your employer makes them, they are not taxable to you (excluded from income and wages). If you contribute, you can deduct those contributions from your taxable income on your tax return.

There is a lot of flexibility on the source of the contributions to your HSA. For instance, your spouse or partner can make them on your behalf. Additionally, you can make one-time transfers from your IRA to an HSA.

The key is that you must keep track of how much goes into your account and make sure it doesn't go over the limit. Your account administrator, trustee, or custodian will not notify you if you exceed your allowable contribution amount. **<u>The management of your deposits and withdrawals is your responsibility.</u>**

You can also make contributions to your HSA in a lump sum or in any amounts or frequency you wish under HSA rules; however, your administrator, who is your account trustee or custodian, may impose requirements. These can include a minimum deposit and minimum balance requirements.

You can make a full year's contribution plus the catch-up, if applicable, to an HSA anytime during the first year you become eligible, as long as you follow two rules:

*Rule #1*— You must be eligible by December 1. In other words, you must have established an HDHP and meet all the other eligibility requirements.

> If you are at least 55-years old, you can make additional catch-up contributions of up to $1,000 per year. And if you and your spouse are 55 or older, both of you can take advantage of the $1,000 catch-up contribution limit whether you have an individual or a family HDHP. Remember though, contributions must stop once you are enrolled in Medicare.

*Rule #2*— If you contribute a full year's contribution, but are eligible only part of the year, you will be subject to taxes and penalties if you don't remain eligible for 12 months after the year in which you first become eligible.

For example, if you become eligible on December 1, 2012 and make a full year's contributions, you will need to remain eligible through all of 2013 to avoid tax and penalties. You can also make a full year's worth of catch-up contributions no matter when your birthday falls during the year.

Sometimes families have multiple HDHP coverage or additional non-HDHP coverage. If you have family coverage, you can contribute the maximum HSA limit for a family. Other coverage of dependent children or your spouse does not affect your contribution limit, except that if your spouse is not eligible, he or she cannot have an HSA.

If one of you has family coverage and the other individual coverage, or even if you both have family coverage, this does not affect your ability to make the maximum family contribution. In these cases, assuming you both have an HSA, you must allocate by agreement between you what amount of the contribution goes towards each HSA.

Be careful with your contribution level each year as you must withdraw excess contributions to the HSA by December 31 or get hit with an excise tax. A pro-rata portion of earnings on the account must be taken out also. The withdrawals will be taxable, but you'll avoid the 20% penalty.

If you did not reach the maximum contribution limit, any other withdrawal that is not for qualified medical expenses for the year will be taxable and subject to a penalty.

You might wonder why you would make an excess contribution, if it is going to be taxed and potentially penalized. One reason could be that you believe your money is better off working for you, tax-free, as part of your HSA investment portfolio during the year. You could then adjust the level to the maximum contribution level, including adjusting for earnings on the contribution, at the end of the year. However, before you make any excess contribution decisions, you should seek appropriate professional guidance.

If you make your contributions through your employer, you can use a salary reduction arrangement with a cafeteria plan, also known as a 125 plan. The amount you contribute can change monthly. And because you are contributing through a cafeteria plan your contributions are pre-tax, meaning they're not subject to individual or employment taxes.

Your employer can also contribute its own money to your HSA. As with your contributions, these are always excluded from your income. Your employer does have to follow some rules.

For example contributions must be comparable for all employees participating in the HSA. If contributions are not comparable, your employer will be liable for additional taxes. Although contributions cannot be greater for higher-paid employees than they are for lower-paid employees, contributions that favor lower paid employees are allowed.

Your employer is not allowed to make additional contributions to an HSA for employees who meet a specified age, qualify for the catch-up contributions, or are based on length of service.

Your employer is permitted to count only eligible employees covered under the HDHP who have the same category of coverage, family or individual. No other classifications of employees are permitted.

Your employer also has limited opportunities to recover contributions:

- If an employer contributes to your account and you were never eligible, that means no HSA ever existed and the employer may recover the funds.

- If your employer's annual contributions to an HSA exceed the maximum allowed due to an error, your employer may correct the error and recover the excess payments.

But your employer may not recoup contributions if:

- Amounts contributed are less than or equal to the maximum annual contribution allowed.

- They are made after you become ineligible, unless the contributions exceed the maximum annual contribution.

## What Happens if I Want to Transfer Money From Another HSA?

An HSA that is funded by amounts rolled over or transferred from an Archer MSA or another HSA is established as of the date the prior account was established.

The only requirement is that your prior HSA had a balance greater than zero at any time during the 18-month period ending on the date the later HSA is established.

When you establish your HSA, you have 60 days to rollover your Archer MSA or other HSA funds. The restrictions follow the IRA rollover rules. Direct trustee to trustee transfers of HSA amounts are not subject to the rollover restrictions but must be agreed by both trustees.

If you are self-employed, a partner in a partnership or an LLC, or an owner or officer with greater than 2% share of a Subchapter S corporation, you are generally not considered an employee. Therefore, you cannot receive an employer contribution to your HSA from that business.

However, suppose you have a second job where you are considered an employee? You could receive employer contributions in respect of that job. You may, of course, make your own personal contributions to your HSA and take deductions on your income taxes.

Contributions are not just limited to your ongoing payments. Rollovers from Archer MSAs and other HSAs are permitted. However, only one rollover per year is allowed and in keeping with restrictions placed on IRA rollovers, a rollover to a new HSA must be completed within 60 days.

Direct rollovers from some plans, such as your 401(k), 403(b) or 457 plan, are not allowed. You may however take withdrawals, subject to the applicable penalties, from your retirement accounts and make contributions to your HSA from them. To make sure you don't end up with any unexpected fees or IRS notices, seek professional advice before removing money from retirement accounts.

you lose your HDHP coverage, you are no longer eligible to contribute to an HSA for the months that you are not covered by an HDHP. If you regain HDHP coverage and remain eligible at a later date, you can begin making contributions to your HSA again. In the interim period you may continue to use your HSA account to meet qualified heath expenses. If you are no longer eligible on the first day of the last month of your tax year, both the HSA contribution and catch-up contribution apply pro rata based on the number of months of the year you are eligible.

## Out-of-Pocket Expenses

The costs to you are the high-deductible health plan premiums, the administrative fees associated with your HSA, and the medical expenses you pay out from your HSA.

You'll probably find that you have to pay some fees to your HSA administrator. HSA trustee or custodian fees can be paid from the assets in the HSA account without being subject to tax or penalty and are not counted toward the HSA contribution limits. Or you can pay them directly without being counted toward the HSA contribution limits.

## Qualifying Expenses

To be a qualifying expense for medical care under IRS rules, the expense has to be primarily for the prevention or alleviation of a physical or mental defect or illness. The key word here is "primarily," as this is often what the IRS uses as its guide during audits of HSA expenses. You can find a partial list of covered medical expenses in IRS Pub 502 http://www.irs.gov/pub/irs-pdf/p502.pdf.

In general, HSA funds can be used to pay for any qualified medical expense regardless of

**Good to Know**

Medical expenses incurred before your HSA is established are not qualified medical expenses and will not count towards your deductible. This is true even if you established your HDHP some months earlier.

whether or not the expense is covered under your HDHP. An example of this would be for nonprescription drugs, such as cough medicine. This would probably not be included under your HDHP (and thus is not counted toward your deductible). But your HSA can be used to pay for it.

Note that beginning in 2013, you will have to get a doctor's prescription for over-the-counter medicine in order for it to be a qualified expense in your HSA (an exception has been made for insulin). Dental and vision care are normally qualified medical expenses under an HSA, but cosmetic procedures, like cosmetic dentistry, are not.

One of the biggest benefits of having an HSA is that you can use the funds to pay for your spouse's or dependent's medical expenses, even if they're not covered by a family HDHP. Another advantage is that in case you have medical expenses in another country, you can use your HSA to cover those expenses, too.

As we mentioned earlier, you cannot continue to contribute to your HSA once you elect to enroll in Medicare. The HSA fund, however, continues to exist and can be used for out-of-pocket health expenses. You can use it to pay Medicare premiums, deductibles, co-payments and coinsurance under any part of Medicare, including Medicare Part D.

Remember that as the HSA owner, if you are 65 or over, this includes your spouse or dependents that might have Medicare.

If you have retiree health benefits through your former employer, you can also use your account to pay your medical insurance premiums. The exceptions are that you cannot pay for a Medicare supplemental insurance (Medigap) policy with your HSA.

You may, however, use your HSA to pay for your spouse or dependent's COBRA premiums no matter what your age is. This exception also covers the premiums for a health plan during a period that you, your spouse or a dependant are receiving unemployment compensation under any Federal or State law.

When you go to the doctor, you will be responsible for 100% of the amount the insurance company agreed to pay until your deductible has been met.

The key is knowing what the agreed upon amount is. After all, you don't want to pay more. Your physician may ask you to pay for the services provided before you leave.

Be sure to ask for the agreed-upon amount so that you're not paying the higher, full stated price.

If your doctor submits the claim directly to the insurance company, you won't be asked to make a payment at the time of your visit.

After the insurance company has processed the claim, you should receive a statement of benefits detailing the total expense, any insurance company discounts, and the amount you need to pay the doctor

Once funds are deposited into the HSA, the account can be used, tax-free, to pay for qualified medical expenses even if you no longer have HDHP coverage. The funds in your account automatically roll over each year and remain indefinitely until used.

You can take tax-free distributions for qualified medical expenses that you, your spouse, a dependent or another person covered by the HDHP may have. And there is no time limit on using the funds.

HSA distributions can even be used to reimburse your prior years' expenses as long as they were incurred on or after the date the HSA was established. There is no time limit on when distributions must occur.

# HDHP Deductibles

You are not required to ensure that all medical expenses paid out of the HSA are charged against the deductible. You may have other coverage for dental or vision care for example, that is a qualified expense but not included in your HDHP deductible.

Although you may use your HSA to make payments on any qualified expense, you cannot count all of these expenses towards your HDHP deductible. Only medical expenses covered by the HDHP may be taken into account in determining whether the HDHP deductible has been met.

How to determine when you can use other coverage in conjunction with your HSA is not as complicated as it might look. You just have to follow the rules. Here's an example ...

Suppose you have individual HDHP coverage with a $2,200 deductible that excludes dental and vision care. And you also have a combination limited purpose and post-deductible health reimbursement account (HRA) through your employer. The HRA pays or reimburses medical expenses after you incur $2,200 in covered medical expenses, and pays or reimburses vision and dental expenses at any time.

You have $2,400 in dental work completed that is reimbursed through your HRA because it is not covered under your HDHP. You then require a small procedure with a dermatologist that is covered under your HDHP. If you have not satisfied your HDHP deductible, you cannot use your HRA to make the payment. You can, however, use your HSA to make the payment as it is a qualified medical expense.

## Distributions and the IRS

Mistaken HSA distributions can be returned to the HSA if you can show clear and convincing evidence that the distribution was a mistake rather than a convenience. The distribution must be repaid by April 15 of the year following the year in which you knew or should have known the distribution was a mistake.

Your HSA trustee must report all distributions annually to you (Form 1099 SA). Then you must file Form 8889 as part of your annual tax return to report the amount of the distribution used for qualified medical expenses.

# Part IV:

# Index of Recommended Health Insurers

Following is a list of recommended health insurers with their Weiss Financial Strength Rating, corporate address, phone number, and the states in which they are licensed. Although this list includes all recommended health insurers identified as licensed to offer a high deductible health plan this does not mean that all of them offer such a product as insurers may change their policy offerings at any time.

# Weiss Recommended Health Insurers by State

The following pages list Weiss Recommended Health Insurers (based strictly on financial strength) licensed to do business in each state. These insurers currently receive a Weiss Financial Strength Rating of A+, A, A-, or B+, indicating their strong financial position. Companies are listed by their Financial Strength Rating and then alphabetically within each Financial Strength Rating grouping.

If an insurer is not on this list, it should not be automatically assumed that the firm is weak. Indeed, there are many firms that have not achieved a B+ or better rating but are in relatively good condition with adequate resources to cover their risk. Not being included in this list should not be construed as a recommendation to cancel a policy.

To get a Weiss Financial Strength Rating for a company not included here, go to www.weissratings.com and click on "Insurers and HMOs".

| | |
|---|---|
| **Weiss Financial Strength Rating** | Our rating is measured on a scale from A to F and considers a wide range of factors. Highly rated companies are, in our opinion, less likely to experience financial difficulties than lower-rated firms. See "What Our Ratings Mean" in the Appendix for a definition of each rating category. |
| **Name** | The insurance company's legally registered name, which can sometimes differ from the name that the company uses for advertising. An insurer's name can be very similar to the name of other companies which may not be on this list, so make sure you note the exact name before contacting your agent. |
| **City, Address, State** | The address of the main office where you can contact the firm for additional information or for the location of local branches and/or registered agents. |
| **Telephone** | The telephone number to call for information on purchasing an insurance policy from the company. |

The following list of recommended Health Insurers by State is based on statutory data provided by SNL Financial LC as of September 30, 2012.

# Alabama

## B+

| Company | City | Address | State | Zip | Telephone |
|---|---|---|---|---|---|
| BLUE CROSS BLUE SHIELD OF ALA | Birmingham | 450 Riverchase Parkway E | AL | 35298 | (205) 988-2100 |
| COVENTRY HEALTH & LIFE INS CO | Dover | 160 Greentree Dr Suite 101 | DE | 19904 | (800) 843-7421 |
| EXPRESS SCRIPTS INS CO | Tempe | 7909 S Hardy Dr | AZ | 85284 | (866) 332-5455 |
| MEDCO CONTAINMENT LIFE INS C | Mechanicsburg | 5010 Ritter Rd Suite 115 | PA | 17055 | (717) 795-9133 |
| VIVA HEALTH INC | Birmingham | 1222 14th Ave S | AL | 35205 | (205) 939-1718 |

# Alaska

## A+

| Company | City | Address | State | Zip | Telephone |
|---|---|---|---|---|---|
| HEALTH CARE SVC CORP A MUT L | Chicago | 300 East Randolph Street | IL | 60601 | (312) 653-6000 |

## A-

| Company | City | Address | State | Zip | Telephone |
|---|---|---|---|---|---|
| PREMERA BLUE CROSS | Mountlake Terrac | 7001 220th St SW | WA | 98043 | (425) 918-4000 |

## B+

| Company | City | Address | State | Zip | Telephone |
|---|---|---|---|---|---|
| MEDCO CONTAINMENT LIFE INS C | Mechanicsburg | 5010 Ritter Rd Suite 115 | PA | 17055 | (717) 795-9133 |

# Arizona

## A+

| Company | City | Address | State | Zip | Telephone |
|---|---|---|---|---|---|
| BLUE CROSS BLUE SHIELD OF ARI | Phoenix | 2444 W Las Palmaritas Dr | AZ | 85021 | (602) 864-4100 |
| HEALTH CARE SVC CORP A MUT L | Chicago | 300 East Randolph Street | IL | 60601 | (312) 653-6000 |

## A-

| Company | City | Address | State | Zip | Telephone |
|---|---|---|---|---|---|
| AETNA HEALTH INC (A PA CORP) | Blue Bell | 980 Jolly Rd | PA | 19422 | (800) 872-3862 |

## B+

| Company | City | Address | State | Zip | Telephone |
|---|---|---|---|---|---|
| BCBSAZ ADVANTAGE | Sun City West | 13950 W Meeker Blvd | AZ | 85375 | (480) 684-7744 |
| COVENTRY HEALTH & LIFE INS CO | Dover | 160 Greentree Dr Suite 101 | DE | 19904 | (800) 843-7421 |
| EXPRESS SCRIPTS INS CO | Tempe | 7909 S Hardy Dr | AZ | 85284 | (866) 332-5455 |
| MEDCO CONTAINMENT LIFE INS C | Mechanicsburg | 5010 Ritter Rd Suite 115 | PA | 17055 | (717) 795-9133 |

# Arkansas

## A+

| Company | City | Address | State | Zip | Telephone |
|---|---|---|---|---|---|
| HEALTH CARE SVC CORP A MUT L | Chicago | 300 East Randolph Street | IL | 60601 | (312) 653-6000 |
| HMO PARTNERS INC | Little Rock | 320 West Capitol | AR | 72203 | (501) 221-1800 |
| USABLE MUTUAL INS CO | Little Rock | 601 S Gaines | AR | 72201 | (501) 378-2000 |

## B+

| Company | City | Address | State | Zip | Telephone |
|---|---|---|---|---|---|
| COVENTRY HEALTH & LIFE INS CO | Dover | 160 Greentree Dr Suite 101 | DE | 19904 | (800) 843-7421 |
| EXPRESS SCRIPTS INS CO | Tempe | 7909 S Hardy Dr | AZ | 85284 | (866) 332-5455 |

# Arkansas (continued)

## B+

| Company | City | Address | State | Zip | Telephone |
|---|---|---|---|---|---|
| MEDCO CONTAINMENT LIFE INS C | Mechanicsburg | 5010 Ritter Rd Suite 115 | PA | 17055 | (717) 795-9133 |

# California

## A+

| Company | City | Address | State | Zip | Telephone |
|---|---|---|---|---|---|
| BLUE CROSS OF CALIFORNIA | Thousand Oaks | 1 Wellpoint Way | CA | 91362 | (805) 557-6655 |

## A

| Company | City | Address | State | Zip | Telephone |
|---|---|---|---|---|---|
| CALIFORNIA PHYSICIANS SERVICE | San Francisco | Fifty Beale St | CA | 94105 | (415) 229-5821 |
| KAISER PERMANENTE INS CO | Oakland | 300 Lakeside Dr 26th Floor | CA | 94612 | (877) 847-7572 |

## A-

| Company | City | Address | State | Zip | Telephone |
|---|---|---|---|---|---|
| CAREMORE HEALTH PLAN | Cerritos | 12900 Park Plaza Dr Suite 150 | CA | 90703 | (562) 741-4340 |
| KAISER FOUNDATION HEALTH PL | Oakland | One Kaiser Plaza | CA | 94612 | (510) 271-5910 |

## B+

| Company | City | Address | State | Zip | Telephone |
|---|---|---|---|---|---|
| EXPRESS SCRIPTS INS CO | Tempe | 7909 S Hardy Dr | AZ | 85284 | (866) 332-5455 |
| MEDCO CONTAINMENT LIFE INS C | Mechanicsburg | 5010 Ritter Rd Suite 115 | PA | 17055 | (717) 795-9133 |

# Colorado

## A+

| Company | City | Address | State | Zip | Telephone |
|---|---|---|---|---|---|
| HEALTH CARE SVC CORP A MUT L | Chicago | 300 East Randolph Street | IL | 60601 | (312) 653-6000 |
| ROCKY MOUNTAIN HEALTH MAIN | Grand Junction | 2775 Crossroads Blvd | CO | 81506 | (970) 244-7760 |

## A

| Company | City | Address | State | Zip | Telephone |
|---|---|---|---|---|---|
| KAISER PERMANENTE INS CO | Oakland | 300 Lakeside Dr 26th Floor | CA | 94612 | (877) 847-7572 |

## A-

| Company | City | Address | State | Zip | Telephone |
|---|---|---|---|---|---|
| AETNA HEALTH INC (A PA CORP) | Blue Bell | 980 Jolly Rd | PA | 19422 | (800) 872-3862 |
| ROCKY MOUNTAIN HOSPITAL & M | Denver | 700 Broadway | CO | 80273 | (303) 831-2131 |
| UNITED CONCORDIA COMPANIES I | Harrisburg | 4401 Deer Path Rd | PA | 17110 | (800) 972-4191 |

## B+

| Company | City | Address | State | Zip | Telephone |
|---|---|---|---|---|---|
| COVENTRY HEALTH & LIFE INS CO | Dover | 160 Greentree Dr Suite 101 | DE | 19904 | (800) 843-7421 |
| EXPRESS SCRIPTS INS CO | Tempe | 7909 S Hardy Dr | AZ | 85284 | (866) 332-5455 |
| KAISER FOUNDATION HP OF CO | Denver | 10350 E Dakota Ave | CO | 80231 | (800) 632-9700 |
| MEDCO CONTAINMENT LIFE INS C | Mechanicsburg | 5010 Ritter Rd Suite 115 | PA | 17055 | (717) 795-9133 |

# Connecticut

## A+

| Company | City | Address | State | Zip | Telephone |
|---|---|---|---|---|---|
| HEALTH CARE SVC CORP A MUT L | Chicago | 300 East Randolph Street | IL | 60601 | (312) 653-6000 |

## A-

| Company | City | Address | State | Zip | Telephone |
|---|---|---|---|---|---|
| AETNA BETTER HEALTH INC (A CT | Middletown | 1000 Middle St | CT | 06457 | (800) 872-3862 |

## B+

| Company | City | Address | State | Zip | Telephone |
|---|---|---|---|---|---|
| ANTHEM HEALTH PLANS INC | North Haven | 370 Bassett Rd | CT | 06473 | (203) 239-4911 |
| CONNECTICARE INC | Farmington | 175 Scott Swamp Rd | CT | 06032 | (860) 674-5700 |
| EXPRESS SCRIPTS INS CO | Tempe | 7909 S Hardy Dr | AZ | 85284 | (866) 332-5455 |
| MEDCO CONTAINMENT LIFE INS C | Mechanicsburg | 5010 Ritter Rd Suite 115 | PA | 17055 | (717) 795-9133 |

# Delaware

## A+

| Company | City | Address | State | Zip | Telephone |
|---|---|---|---|---|---|
| HEALTH CARE SVC CORP A MUT L | Chicago | 300 East Randolph Street | IL | 60601 | (312) 653-6000 |

## A-

| Company | City | Address | State | Zip | Telephone |
|---|---|---|---|---|---|
| AETNA HEALTH INC (A PA CORP) | Blue Bell | 980 Jolly Rd | PA | 19422 | (800) 872-3862 |
| UNITED CONCORDIA LIFE & HEAL | Harrisburg | 4401 Deer Path Rd | PA | 17110 | (717) 260-7081 |

## B+

| Company | City | Address | State | Zip | Telephone |
|---|---|---|---|---|---|
| COVENTRY HEALTH & LIFE INS CO | Dover | 160 Greentree Dr Suite 101 | DE | 19904 | (800) 843-7421 |
| EXPRESS SCRIPTS INS CO | Tempe | 7909 S Hardy Dr | AZ | 85284 | (866) 332-5455 |
| MEDCO CONTAINMENT LIFE INS C | Mechanicsburg | 5010 Ritter Rd Suite 115 | PA | 17055 | (717) 795-9133 |

# District of Columbia

## A+

| Company | City | Address | State | Zip | Telephone |
|---|---|---|---|---|---|
| CAREFIRST BLUECHOICE INC | Washington | 840 First Street NE | DC | 20065 | (202) 479-8000 |
| GROUP HOSP & MEDICAL SERVICE | Washington | 840 First Street NE | DC | 20065 | (202) 479-8000 |
| HEALTH CARE SVC CORP A MUT L | Chicago | 300 East Randolph Street | IL | 60601 | (312) 653-6000 |

## A

| Company | City | Address | State | Zip | Telephone |
|---|---|---|---|---|---|
| KAISER PERMANENTE INS CO | Oakland | 300 Lakeside Dr 26th Floor | CA | 94612 | (877) 847-7572 |

## A-

| Company | City | Address | State | Zip | Telephone |
|---|---|---|---|---|---|
| AETNA HEALTH INC (A PA CORP) | Blue Bell | 980 Jolly Rd | PA | 19422 | (800) 872-3862 |
| UNITED CONCORDIA LIFE & HEAL | Harrisburg | 4401 Deer Path Rd | PA | 17110 | (717) 260-7081 |

## B+

| Company | City | Address | State | Zip | Telephone |
|---|---|---|---|---|---|
| COVENTRY HEALTH & LIFE INS CO | Dover | 160 Greentree Dr Suite 101 | DE | 19904 | (800) 843-7421 |
| EXPRESS SCRIPTS INS CO | Tempe | 7909 S Hardy Dr | AZ | 85284 | (866) 332-5455 |

# District of Columbia (continued)

## B+

| Company | City | Address | State | Zip | Telephone |
|---|---|---|---|---|---|
| MEDCO CONTAINMENT LIFE INS C | Mechanicsburg | 5010 Ritter Rd Suite 115 | PA | 17055 | (717) 795-9133 |

# Florida

## A+

| Company | City | Address | State | Zip | Telephone |
|---|---|---|---|---|---|
| HEALTH CARE SVC CORP A MUT L | Chicago | 300 East Randolph Street | IL | 60601 | (312) 653-6000 |

## A

| Company | City | Address | State | Zip | Telephone |
|---|---|---|---|---|---|
| CAPITAL HEALTH PLAN INC | Tallahassee | 2140 Centerville Place | FL | 32308 | (850) 383-3333 |

## A-

| Company | City | Address | State | Zip | Telephone |
|---|---|---|---|---|---|
| AETNA HEALTH INC (A FLORIDA C | Tampa | 4630 Woodland Corporate Blvd | FL | 33614 | (813) 261-9630 |
| FLORIDA HEALTH CARE PLAN INC. | Holly Hill | 1340 Ridgewood Ave | FL | 32117 | (386) 676-7100 |

## B+

| Company | City | Address | State | Zip | Telephone |
|---|---|---|---|---|---|
| AMERIGROUP FLORIDA INC | Tampa | 4200 W Cypress St | FL | 33607 | (757) 490-6900 |
| AVMED INC | Miami | 9400 S Dadeland Blvd | FL | 33156 | (352) 372-8400 |
| BLUE CROSS & BLUE SHIELD OF FL | Jacksonville | 4800 Deerwood Campus Pkwy | FL | 32246 | (904) 791-6111 |
| COVENTRY HEALTH & LIFE INS CO | Dover | 160 Greentree Dr Suite 101 | DE | 19904 | (800) 843-7421 |
| EXPRESS SCRIPTS INS CO | Tempe | 7909 S Hardy Dr | AZ | 85284 | (866) 332-5455 |
| MEDCO CONTAINMENT LIFE INS C | Mechanicsburg | 5010 Ritter Rd Suite 115 | PA | 17055 | (717) 795-9133 |
| WELLCARE OF FLORIDA INC | Tampa | 8735 Henderson Rd Ren 2 | FL | 33634 | (813) 243-2974 |

# Georgia

## A+

| Company | City | Address | State | Zip | Telephone |
|---|---|---|---|---|---|
| HEALTH CARE SVC CORP A MUT L | Chicago | 300 East Randolph Street | IL | 60601 | (312) 653-6000 |

## A

| Company | City | Address | State | Zip | Telephone |
|---|---|---|---|---|---|
| KAISER PERMANENTE INS CO | Oakland | 300 Lakeside Dr 26th Floor | CA | 94612 | (877) 847-7572 |

## A-

| Company | City | Address | State | Zip | Telephone |
|---|---|---|---|---|---|
| AMGP GEORGIA MANAGED CARE | Atlanta | 303 Perimeter Center N # 400 | GA | 30346 | (757) 473-2721 |
| WELLCARE OF GEORGIA INC | Atlanta | 211 Perimeter Center 8th FLoor | GA | 30346 | (813) 243-2974 |

## B+

| Company | City | Address | State | Zip | Telephone |
|---|---|---|---|---|---|
| BLUE CROSS BLUE SHIELD HEALT | Atlanta | 3350 Peachtree Rd NE | GA | 30326 | (404) 842-8000 |
| COVENTRY HEALTH & LIFE INS CO | Dover | 160 Greentree Dr Suite 101 | DE | 19904 | (800) 843-7421 |
| COVENTRY HEALTH CARE OF GEO | Atlanta | 1100 Circle 75 Pkwy Ste 1400 | GA | 30339 | (678) 202-2100 |
| EXPRESS SCRIPTS INS CO | Tempe | 7909 S Hardy Dr | AZ | 85284 | (866) 332-5455 |
| MEDCO CONTAINMENT LIFE INS C | Mechanicsburg | 5010 Ritter Rd Suite 115 | PA | 17055 | (717) 795-9133 |

# Hawaii

**A+**

| Company | City | Address | State | Zip | Telephone |
|---|---|---|---|---|---|
| ALOHACARE | Honolulu | 1357 Kapiolani Blvd #1250 | HI | 96814 | (808) 973-1650 |

**A**

| Company | City | Address | State | Zip | Telephone |
|---|---|---|---|---|---|
| KAISER PERMANENTE INS CO | Oakland | 300 Lakeside Dr 26th Floor | CA | 94612 | (877) 847-7572 |

**B+**

| Company | City | Address | State | Zip | Telephone |
|---|---|---|---|---|---|
| MEDCO CONTAINMENT LIFE INS C | Mechanicsburg | 5010 Ritter Rd Suite 115 | PA | 17055 | (717) 795-9133 |

# Idaho

**A+**

| Company | City | Address | State | Zip | Telephone |
|---|---|---|---|---|---|
| BLUE CROSS OF IDAHO HEALTH S | Meridian | 3000 E Pine Ave | ID | 83642 | (208) 345-4550 |
| HEALTH CARE SVC CORP A MUT L | Chicago | 300 East Randolph Street | IL | 60601 | (312) 653-6000 |

**A-**

| Company | City | Address | State | Zip | Telephone |
|---|---|---|---|---|---|
| ALTIUS HEALTH PLANS | South Jordan | 10421 S Jordan Gateway Ste 400 | UT | 84095 | (801) 933-3500 |
| SELECTHEALTH INC | Murray | 5381 Green St | UT | 84123 | (801) 442-5000 |

**B+**

| Company | City | Address | State | Zip | Telephone |
|---|---|---|---|---|---|
| MEDCO CONTAINMENT LIFE INS C | Mechanicsburg | 5010 Ritter Rd Suite 115 | PA | 17055 | (717) 795-9133 |

# Illinois

**A+**

| Company | City | Address | State | Zip | Telephone |
|---|---|---|---|---|---|
| HEALTH CARE SVC CORP A MUT L | Chicago | 300 East Randolph Street | IL | 60601 | (312) 653-6000 |

**A-**

| Company | City | Address | State | Zip | Telephone |
|---|---|---|---|---|---|
| AETNA HEALTH INC (A PA CORP) | Blue Bell | 980 Jolly Rd | PA | 19422 | (800) 872-3862 |
| UNITED CONCORDIA LIFE & HEAL | Harrisburg | 4401 Deer Path Rd | PA | 17110 | (717) 260-7081 |

**B+**

| Company | City | Address | State | Zip | Telephone |
|---|---|---|---|---|---|
| COVENTRY HEALTH & LIFE INS CO | Dover | 160 Greentree Dr Suite 101 | DE | 19904 | (800) 843-7421 |
| COVENTRY HEALTH CARE OF ILLI | Champaign | 2110 Fox Dr | IL | 61820 | (217) 366-1226 |
| EXPRESS SCRIPTS INS CO | Tempe | 7909 S Hardy Dr | AZ | 85284 | (866) 332-5455 |
| HARMONY HEALTH PLAN OF ILLIN | Chicago | 200 W Adams St 8th Floor | IL | 60606 | (813) 243-2974 |
| HEALTH ALLIANCE MEDICAL PLA | Urbana | 301 S Vine | IL | 61801 | (217) 337-8406 |
| MEDCO CONTAINMENT LIFE INS C | Mechanicsburg | 5010 Ritter Rd Suite 115 | PA | 17055 | (717) 795-9133 |
| UNITEDHEALTHCARE PLAN RIVER | Moline | 1300 River Drive | IL | 61265 | (309) 736-4600 |

# Indiana

## A+

| Company | City | Address | State | Zip | Telephone |
|---|---|---|---|---|---|
| HEALTH CARE SVC CORP A MUT L | Chicago | 300 East Randolph Street | IL | 60601 | (312) 653-6000 |
| MEDICAL MUTUAL OF OHIO | Cleveland | 2060 E Ninth St | OH | 44115 | (216) 687-7000 |

## A-

| Company | City | Address | State | Zip | Telephone |
|---|---|---|---|---|---|
| AETNA HEALTH INC (A PA CORP) | Blue Bell | 980 Jolly Rd | PA | 19422 | (800) 872-3862 |

## B+

| Company | City | Address | State | Zip | Telephone |
|---|---|---|---|---|---|
| COMMUNITY INS CO | Mason | 4361 Irwin Simpson Rd | OH | 45040 | (513) 872-8100 |
| EXPRESS SCRIPTS INS CO | Tempe | 7909 S Hardy Dr | AZ | 85284 | (866) 332-5455 |
| HARMONY HEALTH PLAN OF ILLIN | Chicago | 200 W Adams St 8th Floor | IL | 60606 | (813) 243-2974 |
| MEDCO CONTAINMENT LIFE INS C | Mechanicsburg | 5010 Ritter Rd Suite 115 | PA | 17055 | (717) 795-9133 |

# Iowa

## B+

| Company | City | Address | State | Zip | Telephone |
|---|---|---|---|---|---|
| COVENTRY HEALTH & LIFE INS CO | Dover | 160 Greentree Dr Suite 101 | DE | 19904 | (800) 843-7421 |
| EXPRESS SCRIPTS INS CO | Tempe | 7909 S Hardy Dr | AZ | 85284 | (866) 332-5455 |
| MEDCO CONTAINMENT LIFE INS C | Mechanicsburg | 5010 Ritter Rd Suite 115 | PA | 17055 | (717) 795-9133 |
| UNITED HEALTHCARE OF THE MID | Omaha | 2717 N. 118th Circle Ste 300 | NE | 68164 | (402) 445-5000 |
| UNITEDHEALTHCARE PLAN RIVER | Moline | 1300 River Drive | IL | 61265 | (309) 736-4600 |
| WELLMARK HEALTH PLAN OF IOW | Des Moines | 636 Grand Ave | IA | 50309 | (515) 245-4500 |

# Kansas

## A+

| Company | City | Address | State | Zip | Telephone |
|---|---|---|---|---|---|
| BLUE CROSS BLUE SHIELD OF KC | Kansas City | 2301 Main St | MO | 64108 | (816) 395-2222 |

## A

| Company | City | Address | State | Zip | Telephone |
|---|---|---|---|---|---|
| GOOD HEALTH HMO INC | Kansas City | 2301 Main St | MO | 64108 | (816) 395-2222 |

## A-

| Company | City | Address | State | Zip | Telephone |
|---|---|---|---|---|---|
| AETNA HEALTH INC (A PA CORP) | Blue Bell | 980 Jolly Rd | PA | 19422 | (800) 872-3862 |
| HEALTHY ALLIANCE LIFE INS CO | St Louis | 1831 Chestnut St | MO | 63103 | (314) 923-4444 |

## B+

| Company | City | Address | State | Zip | Telephone |
|---|---|---|---|---|---|
| COVENTRY HEALTH & LIFE INS CO | Dover | 160 Greentree Dr Suite 101 | DE | 19904 | (800) 843-7421 |
| MEDCO CONTAINMENT LIFE INS C | Mechanicsburg | 5010 Ritter Rd Suite 115 | PA | 17055 | (717) 795-9133 |

# Kentucky

## A+

| Company | City | Address | State | Zip | Telephone |
|---|---|---|---|---|---|
| HEALTH CARE SVC CORP A MUT L | Chicago | 300 East Randolph Street | IL | 60601 | (312) 653-6000 |

## Kentucky (continued)

### A-

| Company | City | Address | State | Zip | Telephone |
|---|---|---|---|---|---|
| AETNA HEALTH INC (A PA CORP) | Blue Bell | 980 Jolly Rd | PA | 19422 | (800) 872-3862 |
| UNITED CONCORDIA LIFE & HEAL | Harrisburg | 4401 Deer Path Rd | PA | 17110 | (717) 260-7081 |

### B+

| Company | City | Address | State | Zip | Telephone |
|---|---|---|---|---|---|
| ANTHEM HEALTH PLANS OF KENT | Louisville | 13550 Triton Park Blvd | KY | 40223 | (502) 423-2011 |
| COVENTRY HEALTH & LIFE INS CO | Dover | 160 Greentree Dr Suite 101 | DE | 19904 | (800) 843-7421 |
| EXPRESS SCRIPTS INS CO | Tempe | 7909 S Hardy Dr | AZ | 85284 | (866) 332-5455 |
| MEDCO CONTAINMENT LIFE INS C | Mechanicsburg | 5010 Ritter Rd Suite 115 | PA | 17055 | (717) 795-9133 |
| UNIVERSITY HEALTH CARE INC | Louisville | 305 W Broadway Ave 3rd Floor | KY | 40202 | (502) 852-5872 |

## Louisiana

### A+

| Company | City | Address | State | Zip | Telephone |
|---|---|---|---|---|---|
| HMO LOUISIANA INC | Baton Rouge | 5525 Reitz Ave | LA | 70809 | (225) 295-3307 |
| LA HEALTH SERVICE & INDEMNIT | Baton Rouge | 5525 Reitz Ave | LA | 70809 | (225) 295-3307 |

### B+

| Company | City | Address | State | Zip | Telephone |
|---|---|---|---|---|---|
| COVENTRY HEALTH & LIFE INS CO | Dover | 160 Greentree Dr Suite 101 | DE | 19904 | (800) 843-7421 |
| EXPRESS SCRIPTS INS CO | Tempe | 7909 S Hardy Dr | AZ | 85284 | (866) 332-5455 |
| MEDCO CONTAINMENT LIFE INS C | Mechanicsburg | 5010 Ritter Rd Suite 115 | PA | 17055 | (717) 795-9133 |

## Maine

### A+

| Company | City | Address | State | Zip | Telephone |
|---|---|---|---|---|---|
| HEALTH CARE SVC CORP A MUT L | Chicago | 300 East Randolph Street | IL | 60601 | (312) 653-6000 |

### A

| Company | City | Address | State | Zip | Telephone |
|---|---|---|---|---|---|
| HARVARD PILGRIM HEALTH CARE | Wellesley | 93 Worcester St | MA | 02481 | (617) 509-5697 |

### A-

| Company | City | Address | State | Zip | Telephone |
|---|---|---|---|---|---|
| ANTHEM HEALTH PLANS OF MAIN | S Portland | 2 Gannett Cr | ME | 04106 | (207) 822-7000 |

### B+

| Company | City | Address | State | Zip | Telephone |
|---|---|---|---|---|---|
| COVENTRY HEALTH & LIFE INS CO | Dover | 160 Greentree Dr Suite 101 | DE | 19904 | (800) 843-7421 |
| EXPRESS SCRIPTS INS CO | Tempe | 7909 S Hardy Dr | AZ | 85284 | (866) 332-5455 |
| MEDCO CONTAINMENT LIFE INS C | Mechanicsburg | 5010 Ritter Rd Suite 115 | PA | 17055 | (717) 795-9133 |

## Maryland

### A+

| Company | City | Address | State | Zip | Telephone |
|---|---|---|---|---|---|
| CAREFIRST BLUECHOICE INC | Washington | 840 First Street NE | DC | 20065 | (202) 479-8000 |
| GROUP HOSP & MEDICAL SERVICE | Washington | 840 First Street NE | DC | 20065 | (202) 479-8000 |

# Maryland (continued)

### A+

| Company | City | Address | State | Zip | Telephone |
|---|---|---|---|---|---|
| HEALTH CARE SVC CORP A MUT L | Chicago | 300 East Randolph Street | IL | 60601 | (312) 653-6000 |

### A

| Company | City | Address | State | Zip | Telephone |
|---|---|---|---|---|---|
| KAISER PERMANENTE INS CO | Oakland | 300 Lakeside Dr 26th Floor | CA | 94612 | (877) 847-7572 |

### A-

| Company | City | Address | State | Zip | Telephone |
|---|---|---|---|---|---|
| AETNA HEALTH INC (A PA CORP) | Blue Bell | 980 Jolly Rd | PA | 19422 | (800) 872-3862 |
| AMERIGROUP MARYLAND INC | Hanover | 7550 Teague Rd Suite 500 | MD | 21076 | (757) 490-6900 |
| UNITED CONCORDIA LIFE & HEAL | Harrisburg | 4401 Deer Path Rd | PA | 17110 | (717) 260-7081 |

### B+

| Company | City | Address | State | Zip | Telephone |
|---|---|---|---|---|---|
| COVENTRY HEALTH & LIFE INS CO | Dover | 160 Greentree Dr Suite 101 | DE | 19904 | (800) 843-7421 |
| EXPRESS SCRIPTS INS CO | Tempe | 7909 S Hardy Dr | AZ | 85284 | (866) 332-5455 |
| MEDCO CONTAINMENT LIFE INS C | Mechanicsburg | 5010 Ritter Rd Suite 115 | PA | 17055 | (717) 795-9133 |

# Massachusetts

### A+

| Company | City | Address | State | Zip | Telephone |
|---|---|---|---|---|---|
| HEALTH CARE SVC CORP A MUT L | Chicago | 300 East Randolph Street | IL | 60601 | (312) 653-6000 |

### A

| Company | City | Address | State | Zip | Telephone |
|---|---|---|---|---|---|
| HARVARD PILGRIM HEALTH CARE | Wellesley | 93 Worcester St | MA | 02481 | (617) 509-5697 |
| HEALTH NEW ENGLAND INC | Springfield | 1 Monarch Pl, Ste 1500 | MA | 01144 | (413) 787-4000 |

### A-

| Company | City | Address | State | Zip | Telephone |
|---|---|---|---|---|---|
| AETNA HEALTH INC (A PA CORP) | Blue Bell | 980 Jolly Rd | PA | 19422 | (800) 872-3862 |

### B+

| Company | City | Address | State | Zip | Telephone |
|---|---|---|---|---|---|
| BLUE CROSS BLUE SHIELD OF MA | Boston | 401 Park Dr | MA | 02215 | (617) 246-5000 |
| EXPRESS SCRIPTS INS CO | Tempe | 7909 S Hardy Dr | AZ | 85284 | (866) 332-5455 |
| MEDCO CONTAINMENT LIFE INS C | Mechanicsburg | 5010 Ritter Rd Suite 115 | PA | 17055 | (717) 795-9133 |

# Michigan

### A+

| Company | City | Address | State | Zip | Telephone |
|---|---|---|---|---|---|
| HEALTH CARE SVC CORP A MUT L | Chicago | 300 East Randolph Street | IL | 60601 | (312) 653-6000 |
| MEDICAL MUTUAL OF OHIO | Cleveland | 2060 E Ninth St | OH | 44115 | (216) 687-7000 |

### A

| Company | City | Address | State | Zip | Telephone |
|---|---|---|---|---|---|
| HEALTHPLUS OF MICHIGAN | Flint | 2050 S Linden Rd | MI | 48532 | (810) 332-9161 |

## Michigan (continued)

### A-

| Company | City | Address | State | Zip | Telephone |
|---|---|---|---|---|---|
| BLUE CARE NETWORK OF MICHIG | Southfield | 20500 Civic Center Drive | MI | 48076 | (248) 799-6400 |

### B+

| Company | City | Address | State | Zip | Telephone |
|---|---|---|---|---|---|
| BLUE CROSS BLUE SHIELD OF MIC | Detroit | 600 Lafayette East | MI | 48226 | (313) 225-9000 |
| COVENTRY HEALTH & LIFE INS CO | Dover | 160 Greentree Dr Suite 101 | DE | 19904 | (800) 843-7421 |
| EXPRESS SCRIPTS INS CO | Tempe | 7909 S Hardy Dr | AZ | 85284 | (866) 332-5455 |
| HEALTH ALLIANCE PLAN OF MICH | Detroit | 2850 W Grand Blvd | MI | 48202 | (313) 872-8100 |
| MEDCO CONTAINMENT LIFE INS C | Mechanicsburg | 5010 Ritter Rd Suite 115 | PA | 17055 | (717) 795-9133 |

## Minnesota

### A+

| Company | City | Address | State | Zip | Telephone |
|---|---|---|---|---|---|
| BLUE CROSS BLUE SHIELD OF MIN | Eagan | 3535 Blue Cross Rd | MN | 55122 | (651) 662-8000 |
| HEALTH CARE SVC CORP A MUT L | Chicago | 300 East Randolph Street | IL | 60601 | (312) 653-6000 |

### A

| Company | City | Address | State | Zip | Telephone |
|---|---|---|---|---|---|
| MEDICA HEALTH PLANS | Minnetonka | 401 Carlson Parkway | MN | 55305 | (952) 992-2900 |

### A-

| Company | City | Address | State | Zip | Telephone |
|---|---|---|---|---|---|
| HEALTHPARTNERS INS CO | Minneapolis | 8170 33rd Ave S | MN | 55440 | (952) 883-6000 |
| HMO MINNESOTA | St Paul | 3535 Blue Cross Rd, 43179 | MN | 55164 | (651) 662-8000 |
| MEDICA INS CO | Minnetonka | 401 Carlson Parkway | MN | 55305 | (952) 992-2900 |
| NORIDIAN MUTUAL INS CO | Fargo | 4510 13th Ave S | ND | 58121 | (701) 282-1100 |
| UCARE MINNESOTA | Minneapolis | 500 Stinson Blvd NE | MN | 55413 | (612) 676-6500 |

### B+

| Company | City | Address | State | Zip | Telephone |
|---|---|---|---|---|---|
| EXPRESS SCRIPTS INS CO | Tempe | 7909 S Hardy Dr | AZ | 85284 | (866) 332-5455 |
| MEDCO CONTAINMENT LIFE INS C | Mechanicsburg | 5010 Ritter Rd Suite 115 | PA | 17055 | (717) 795-9133 |
| PREFERREDONE INS CO | Golden Valley | 6105 Golden Hills Dr | MN | 55416 | (763) 847-4000 |

## Mississippi

### A-

| Company | City | Address | State | Zip | Telephone |
|---|---|---|---|---|---|
| BLUE CROSS BLUE SHIELD OF MS, | Flowood | 3545 Lakeland Dr | MS | 39208 | (601) 932-3704 |

### B+

| Company | City | Address | State | Zip | Telephone |
|---|---|---|---|---|---|
| COVENTRY HEALTH & LIFE INS CO | Dover | 160 Greentree Dr Suite 101 | DE | 19904 | (800) 843-7421 |
| EXPRESS SCRIPTS INS CO | Tempe | 7909 S Hardy Dr | AZ | 85284 | (866) 332-5455 |
| MEDCO CONTAINMENT LIFE INS C | Mechanicsburg | 5010 Ritter Rd Suite 115 | PA | 17055 | (717) 795-9133 |

# Missouri

## A+

| Company | City | Address | State | Zip | Telephone |
|---|---|---|---|---|---|
| BLUE CROSS BLUE SHIELD OF KC | Kansas City | 2301 Main St | MO | 64108 | (816) 395-2222 |
| HEALTH CARE SVC CORP A MUT L | Chicago | 300 East Randolph Street | IL | 60601 | (312) 653-6000 |

## A

| Company | City | Address | State | Zip | Telephone |
|---|---|---|---|---|---|
| GOOD HEALTH HMO INC | Kansas City | 2301 Main St | MO | 64108 | (816) 395-2222 |

## A-

| Company | City | Address | State | Zip | Telephone |
|---|---|---|---|---|---|
| AETNA HEALTH INC (A PA CORP) | Blue Bell | 980 Jolly Rd | PA | 19422 | (800) 872-3862 |
| HEALTHY ALLIANCE LIFE INS CO | St Louis | 1831 Chestnut St | MO | 63103 | (314) 923-4444 |
| UNITED CONCORDIA LIFE & HEAL | Harrisburg | 4401 Deer Path Rd | PA | 17110 | (717) 260-7081 |

## B+

| Company | City | Address | State | Zip | Telephone |
|---|---|---|---|---|---|
| COVENTRY HEALTH & LIFE INS CO | Dover | 160 Greentree Dr Suite 101 | DE | 19904 | (800) 843-7421 |
| EXPRESS SCRIPTS INS CO | Tempe | 7909 S Hardy Dr | AZ | 85284 | (866) 332-5455 |
| HARMONY HEALTH PLAN OF ILLIN | Chicago | 200 W Adams St 8th Floor | IL | 60606 | (813) 243-2974 |
| MEDCO CONTAINMENT LIFE INS C | Mechanicsburg | 5010 Ritter Rd Suite 115 | PA | 17055 | (717) 795-9133 |

# Montana

## A+

| Company | City | Address | State | Zip | Telephone |
|---|---|---|---|---|---|
| HEALTH CARE SVC CORP A MUT L | Chicago | 300 East Randolph Street | IL | 60601 | (312) 653-6000 |

## B+

| Company | City | Address | State | Zip | Telephone |
|---|---|---|---|---|---|
| EXPRESS SCRIPTS INS CO | Tempe | 7909 S Hardy Dr | AZ | 85284 | (866) 332-5455 |
| MEDCO CONTAINMENT LIFE INS C | Mechanicsburg | 5010 Ritter Rd Suite 115 | PA | 17055 | (717) 795-9133 |

# Nebraska

## A+

| Company | City | Address | State | Zip | Telephone |
|---|---|---|---|---|---|
| HEALTH CARE SVC CORP A MUT L | Chicago | 300 East Randolph Street | IL | 60601 | (312) 653-6000 |

## A-

| Company | City | Address | State | Zip | Telephone |
|---|---|---|---|---|---|
| BLUE CROSS BLUE SHIELD OF NEB | Omaha | 7261 Mercy Rd | NE | 68124 | (402) 390-1800 |

## B+

| Company | City | Address | State | Zip | Telephone |
|---|---|---|---|---|---|
| COVENTRY HEALTH & LIFE INS CO | Dover | 160 Greentree Dr Suite 101 | DE | 19904 | (800) 843-7421 |
| MEDCO CONTAINMENT LIFE INS C | Mechanicsburg | 5010 Ritter Rd Suite 115 | PA | 17055 | (717) 795-9133 |
| UNITED HEALTHCARE OF THE MID | Omaha | 2717 N. 118th Circle Ste 300 | NE | 68164 | (402) 445-5000 |

# Nevada

### A+

| Company | City | Address | State | Zip | Telephone |
|---|---|---|---|---|---|
| HEALTH CARE SVC CORP A MUT L | Chicago | 300 East Randolph Street | IL | 60601 | (312) 653-6000 |

### A-

| Company | City | Address | State | Zip | Telephone |
|---|---|---|---|---|---|
| AETNA HEALTH INC (A PA CORP) | Blue Bell | 980 Jolly Rd | PA | 19422 | (800) 872-3862 |
| ROCKY MOUNTAIN HOSPITAL & M | Denver | 700 Broadway | CO | 80273 | (303) 831-2131 |

### B+

| Company | City | Address | State | Zip | Telephone |
|---|---|---|---|---|---|
| COVENTRY HEALTH & LIFE INS CO | Dover | 160 Greentree Dr Suite 101 | DE | 19904 | (800) 843-7421 |
| MEDCO CONTAINMENT LIFE INS C | Mechanicsburg | 5010 Ritter Rd Suite 115 | PA | 17055 | (717) 795-9133 |

# New Hampshire

### A+

| Company | City | Address | State | Zip | Telephone |
|---|---|---|---|---|---|
| HEALTH CARE SVC CORP A MUT L | Chicago | 300 East Randolph Street | IL | 60601 | (312) 653-6000 |

### B+

| Company | City | Address | State | Zip | Telephone |
|---|---|---|---|---|---|
| ANTHEM HEALTH PLANS OF NEW | Mancheter | 3000 Goffs Falls Rd | NH | 03111 | (603) 695-7000 |
| EXPRESS SCRIPTS INS CO | Tempe | 7909 S Hardy Dr | AZ | 85284 | (866) 332-5455 |
| MEDCO CONTAINMENT LIFE INS C | Mechanicsburg | 5010 Ritter Rd Suite 115 | PA | 17055 | (717) 795-9133 |

# New Jersey

### A+

| Company | City | Address | State | Zip | Telephone |
|---|---|---|---|---|---|
| HEALTH CARE SVC CORP A MUT L | Chicago | 300 East Randolph Street | IL | 60601 | (312) 653-6000 |

### A

| Company | City | Address | State | Zip | Telephone |
|---|---|---|---|---|---|
| AMERIGROUP NEW JERSEY INC | Edison | 399 Thomall St., 9th Floor | NJ | 08818 | (757) 490-6900 |
| HORIZON HEALTHCARE OF NEW J | Newark | 3 Penn Plaza East- PP-15D | NJ | 07105 | (973) 466-8600 |

### A-

| Company | City | Address | State | Zip | Telephone |
|---|---|---|---|---|---|
| BRAVO HEALTH PENNSYLVANIA I | Philadelphia | 1500 Spring Garden St Ste 80 | PA | 19130 | (800) 235-9188 |
| UNITED CONCORDIA LIFE & HEAL | Harrisburg | 4401 Deer Path Rd | PA | 17110 | (717) 260-7081 |

### B+

| Company | City | Address | State | Zip | Telephone |
|---|---|---|---|---|---|
| EXPRESS SCRIPTS INS CO | Tempe | 7909 S Hardy Dr | AZ | 85284 | (866) 332-5455 |
| MEDCO CONTAINMENT LIFE INS C | Mechanicsburg | 5010 Ritter Rd Suite 115 | PA | 17055 | (717) 795-9133 |
| OXFORD HEALTH PLANS (NJ) INC | Iselin | 111 Wood Ave S Ste 2 | NJ | 08837 | (203) 459-6000 |

# New Mexico

## A+

| Company | City | Address | State | Zip | Telephone |
|---------|------|---------|-------|-----|-----------|
| HEALTH CARE SVC CORP A MUT L | Chicago | 300 East Randolph Street | IL | 60601 | (312) 653-6000 |

## A-

| Company | City | Address | State | Zip | Telephone |
|---------|------|---------|-------|-----|-----------|
| PRESBYTERIAN HEALTH PLAN INC | Albuquerque | 2301 Buena Vista SE | NM | 87106 | (505) 923-5700 |

## B+

| Company | City | Address | State | Zip | Telephone |
|---------|------|---------|-------|-----|-----------|
| MEDCO CONTAINMENT LIFE INS C | Mechanicsburg | 5010 Ritter Rd Suite 115 | PA | 17055 | (717) 795-9133 |
| PRESBYTERIAN INS CO INC | Albuquerque | 2301 Buena Vista Dr SE | NM | 87106 | (505) 923-8311 |

# New York

## A+

| Company | City | Address | State | Zip | Telephone |
|---------|------|---------|-------|-----|-----------|
| CAPITAL DISTRICT PHYSICIANS H | Albany | 500 Patroon Creek Blvd | NY | 12206 | (518) 641-3000 |
| EXCELLUS HEALTH PLAN INC | Rochester | 165 Court St | NY | 14647 | (585) 454-1700 |
| OXFORD HEALTH PLANS (NY) INC | New York | Two Penn Plaza | NY | 10121 | (203) 459-6000 |

## A

| Company | City | Address | State | Zip | Telephone |
|---------|------|---------|-------|-----|-----------|
| HEALTHNOW NY INC | Buffalo | 257 W Genesee St | NY | 14202 | (716) 887-6900 |
| INDEPENDENT HEALTH ASSOC INC | Buffalo | 511 Farber Lakes Dr | NY | 14221 | (716) 635-3939 |

## A-

| Company | City | Address | State | Zip | Telephone |
|---------|------|---------|-------|-----|-----------|
| AETNA HEALTH INC (A NEW YORK | Uniondale | 333 Earle Ovington Blvd #502 | NY | 11553 | (800) 872-3862 |
| EMPIRE HEALTHCHOICE HMO INC | New York | 1 Liberty Plaza 165 Broadway | NY | 10006 | (212) 476-1000 |

## B+

| Company | City | Address | State | Zip | Telephone |
|---------|------|---------|-------|-----|-----------|
| EMPIRE HEALTHCHOICE ASSURAN | New York | 1 Liberty Plaza 165 Broadway | NY | 10006 | (212) 476-1000 |
| EXPRESS SCRIPTS INS CO | Tempe | 7909 S Hardy Dr | AZ | 85284 | (866) 332-5455 |
| HEALTH INSURANCE PLAN OF GRE | New York | 55 Water Street | NY | 10041 | (646) 447-5000 |
| MANAGED HEALTH INC | New York | 25 Broadway, 9th Floor | NY | 10004 | (212) 801-6000 |
| MEDCO CONTAINMENT INS CO OF | Clifton Park | 648 Plank Rd Suite 202 | NY | 12065 | (800) 426-0152 |
| UNITED HEALTHCARE OF NY INC | New York | One Penn Plaza Ste 800 | NY | 10119 | (203) 459-6000 |

# North Carolina

## A+

| Company | City | Address | State | Zip | Telephone |
|---------|------|---------|-------|-----|-----------|
| BLUE CROSS BLUE SHIELD OF NC | Durham | 5901 Chapel Hill Blvd | NC | 27707 | (919) 489-7431 |

## A-

| Company | City | Address | State | Zip | Telephone |
|---------|------|---------|-------|-----|-----------|
| AETNA HEALTH INC (A PA CORP) | Blue Bell | 980 Jolly Rd | PA | 19422 | (800) 872-3862 |
| UNITED CONCORDIA LIFE & HEAL | Harrisburg | 4401 Deer Path Rd | PA | 17110 | (717) 260-7081 |

# North Carolina (continued)

**B+**

| Company | City | Address | State | Zip | Telephone |
| --- | --- | --- | --- | --- | --- |
| COVENTRY HEALTH & LIFE INS CO | Dover | 160 Greentree Dr Suite 101 | DE | 19904 | (800) 843-7421 |
| EXPRESS SCRIPTS INS CO | Tempe | 7909 S Hardy Dr | AZ | 85284 | (866) 332-5455 |
| FIRSTCAROLINACARE INS CO INC | Pinehurst | 42 Memorial Dr Suite 1 | NC | 28374 | (910) 715-8100 |
| MEDCO CONTAINMENT LIFE INS C | Mechanicsburg | 5010 Ritter Rd Suite 115 | PA | 17055 | (717) 795-9133 |

# North Dakota

**A**

| Company | City | Address | State | Zip | Telephone |
| --- | --- | --- | --- | --- | --- |
| MEDICA HEALTH PLANS | Minnetonka | 401 Carlson Parkway | MN | 55305 | (952) 992-2900 |

**A-**

| Company | City | Address | State | Zip | Telephone |
| --- | --- | --- | --- | --- | --- |
| MEDICA INS CO | Minnetonka | 401 Carlson Parkway | MN | 55305 | (952) 992-2900 |
| NORIDIAN MUTUAL INS CO | Fargo | 4510 13th Ave S | ND | 58121 | (701) 282-1100 |

**B+**

| Company | City | Address | State | Zip | Telephone |
| --- | --- | --- | --- | --- | --- |
| MEDCO CONTAINMENT LIFE INS C | Mechanicsburg | 5010 Ritter Rd Suite 115 | PA | 17055 | (717) 795-9133 |

# Ohio

**A+**

| Company | City | Address | State | Zip | Telephone |
| --- | --- | --- | --- | --- | --- |
| HEALTH CARE SVC CORP A MUT L | Chicago | 300 East Randolph Street | IL | 60601 | (312) 653-6000 |
| MEDICAL MUTUAL OF OHIO | Cleveland | 2060 E Ninth St | OH | 44115 | (216) 687-7000 |

**A**

| Company | City | Address | State | Zip | Telephone |
| --- | --- | --- | --- | --- | --- |
| KAISER PERMANENTE INS CO | Oakland | 300 Lakeside Dr 26th Floor | CA | 94612 | (877) 847-7572 |
| MOUNT CARMEL HEALTH PLAN IN | Columbus | 8150 E Broad St EE320 | OH | 43213 | (614) 546-3151 |

**A-**

| Company | City | Address | State | Zip | Telephone |
| --- | --- | --- | --- | --- | --- |
| AETNA HEALTH INC (A PA CORP) | Blue Bell | 980 Jolly Rd | PA | 19422 | (800) 872-3862 |
| CARESOURCE | Dayton | One South Main St, Ste 440 | OH | 45402 | (937) 531-3300 |

**B+**

| Company | City | Address | State | Zip | Telephone |
| --- | --- | --- | --- | --- | --- |
| COMMUNITY INS CO | Mason | 4361 Irwin Simpson Rd | OH | 45040 | (513) 872-8100 |
| COVENTRY HEALTH & LIFE INS CO | Dover | 160 Greentree Dr Suite 101 | DE | 19904 | (800) 843-7421 |
| EXPRESS SCRIPTS INS CO | Tempe | 7909 S Hardy Dr | AZ | 85284 | (866) 332-5455 |
| HEALTH PLAN OF THE UPPER OHI | St Clairsville | 52160 National Rd E | OH | 43950 | (740) 695-3585 |
| MEDCO CONTAINMENT LIFE INS C | Mechanicsburg | 5010 Ritter Rd Suite 115 | PA | 17055 | (717) 795-9133 |
| MEDICAL HEALTH INS CORP OF O | Cleveland | 2060 E Ninth St | OH | 44115 | (216) 687-7000 |
| PARAMOUNT ADVANTAGE | Maumee | 1901 Indian Wood Cir | OH | 43537 | (419) 887-2500 |

# Oklahoma

## A+

| Company | City | Address | State | Zip | Telephone |
|---|---|---|---|---|---|
| HEALTH CARE SVC CORP A MUT L | Chicago | 300 East Randolph Street | IL | 60601 | (312) 653-6000 |

## A

| Company | City | Address | State | Zip | Telephone |
|---|---|---|---|---|---|
| COMMUNITYCARE HMO INC | Tulsa | 218 W. 6th Street | OK | 74119 | (918) 549-5200 |

## A-

| Company | City | Address | State | Zip | Telephone |
|---|---|---|---|---|---|
| AETNA HEALTH INC (A PA CORP) | Blue Bell | 980 Jolly Rd | PA | 19422 | (800) 872-3862 |

## B+

| Company | City | Address | State | Zip | Telephone |
|---|---|---|---|---|---|
| COVENTRY HEALTH & LIFE INS CO | Dover | 160 Greentree Dr Suite 101 | DE | 19904 | (800) 843-7421 |
| EXPRESS SCRIPTS INS CO | Tempe | 7909 S Hardy Dr | AZ | 85284 | (866) 332-5455 |
| MEDCO CONTAINMENT LIFE INS C | Mechanicsburg | 5010 Ritter Rd Suite 115 | PA | 17055 | (717) 795-9133 |

# Oregon

## A+

| Company | City | Address | State | Zip | Telephone |
|---|---|---|---|---|---|
| HEALTH CARE SVC CORP A MUT L | Chicago | 300 East Randolph Street | IL | 60601 | (312) 653-6000 |
| PROVIDENCE HEALTH PLAN | Beaverton | 3601 SW Murray Blvd Ste 10 | OR | 97005 | (503) 574-7500 |

## A

| Company | City | Address | State | Zip | Telephone |
|---|---|---|---|---|---|
| KAISER PERMANENTE INS CO | Oakland | 300 Lakeside Dr 26th Floor | CA | 94612 | (877) 847-7572 |

## A-

| Company | City | Address | State | Zip | Telephone |
|---|---|---|---|---|---|
| KAISER FOUNDATION HP NORTHW | Portland | 500 NE Multnomah St, Suite 100 | OR | 97232 | (503) 813-2800 |

## B+

| Company | City | Address | State | Zip | Telephone |
|---|---|---|---|---|---|
| EXPRESS SCRIPTS INS CO | Tempe | 7909 S Hardy Dr | AZ | 85284 | (866) 332-5455 |
| MEDCO CONTAINMENT LIFE INS C | Mechanicsburg | 5010 Ritter Rd Suite 115 | PA | 17055 | (717) 795-9133 |
| REGENCE BL CROSS BL SHIELD OR | Portland | 100 SW Market St | OR | 97201 | (503) 225-5221 |

# Pennsylvania

## A+

| Company | City | Address | State | Zip | Telephone |
|---|---|---|---|---|---|
| HEALTH CARE SVC CORP A MUT L | Chicago | 300 East Randolph Street | IL | 60601 | (312) 653-6000 |

## A-

| Company | City | Address | State | Zip | Telephone |
|---|---|---|---|---|---|
| AETNA HEALTH INC (A PA CORP) | Blue Bell | 980 Jolly Rd | PA | 19422 | (800) 872-3862 |
| BRAVO HEALTH PENNSYLVANIA I | Philadelphia | 1500 Spring Garden St Ste 80 | PA | 19130 | (800) 235-9188 |
| KEYSTONE HEALTH PLAN WEST IN | Pittsburgh | 120 Fifth Ave | PA | 15222 | (412) 544-7000 |
| UNITED CONCORDIA LIFE & HEAL | Harrisburg | 4401 Deer Path Rd | PA | 17110 | (717) 260-7081 |
| UPMC FOR YOU INC | Pittsburgh | 112 Washington Pl | PA | 15219 | (412) 434-1200 |

# Pennsylvania (continued)

## B+

| Company | City | Address | State | Zip | Telephone |
|---|---|---|---|---|---|
| COVENTRY HEALTH & LIFE INS CO | Dover | 160 Greentree Dr Suite 101 | DE | 19904 | (800) 843-7421 |
| EXPRESS SCRIPTS INS CO | Tempe | 7909 S Hardy Dr | AZ | 85284 | (866) 332-5455 |
| HEALTHASSURANCE PENNSYLVA | Harrisburg | 3721 Tecport Dr. PO Box 67103 | PA | 17106 | (800) 788-6445 |
| KEYSTONE HEALTH PLAN EAST IN | Philadelphia | 1901 Market St | PA | 19101 | (215) 241-2400 |
| MEDCO CONTAINMENT LIFE INS C | Mechanicsburg | 5010 Ritter Rd Suite 115 | PA | 17055 | (717) 795-9133 |
| UPMC HEALTH NETWORK INC | Pittsburgh | 112 Washington Pl | PA | 15219 | (412) 434-1200 |

# Puerto Rico

## A-

| Company | City | Address | State | Zip | Telephone |
|---|---|---|---|---|---|
| TRIPLE-S SALUD INC | San Juan | F D Roosevelt Ave 1441 | PR | 00920 | (787) 749-4949 |

## B+

| Company | City | Address | State | Zip | Telephone |
|---|---|---|---|---|---|
| MEDCO CONTAINMENT LIFE INS C | Mechanicsburg | 5010 Ritter Rd Suite 115 | PA | 17055 | (717) 795-9133 |

# Rhode Island

## B+

| Company | City | Address | State | Zip | Telephone |
|---|---|---|---|---|---|
| EXPRESS SCRIPTS INS CO | Tempe | 7909 S Hardy Dr | AZ | 85284 | (866) 332-5455 |
| MEDCO CONTAINMENT LIFE INS C | Mechanicsburg | 5010 Ritter Rd Suite 115 | PA | 17055 | (717) 795-9133 |

# South Carolina

## A+

| Company | City | Address | State | Zip | Telephone |
|---|---|---|---|---|---|
| HEALTH CARE SVC CORP A MUT L | Chicago | 300 East Randolph Street | IL | 60601 | (312) 653-6000 |

## A

| Company | City | Address | State | Zip | Telephone |
|---|---|---|---|---|---|
| BLUECHOICE HEALTHPLAN OF SC | Columbia | I-20 at Alpine Rd | SC | 29219 | (803) 786-8466 |

## A-

| Company | City | Address | State | Zip | Telephone |
|---|---|---|---|---|---|
| BLUE CROSS BLUE SHIELD OF SC I | Columbia | 2501 Faraway Dr | SC | 29219 | (803) 788-3860 |

## B+

| Company | City | Address | State | Zip | Telephone |
|---|---|---|---|---|---|
| COVENTRY HEALTH & LIFE INS CO | Dover | 160 Greentree Dr Suite 101 | DE | 19904 | (800) 843-7421 |
| EXPRESS SCRIPTS INS CO | Tempe | 7909 S Hardy Dr | AZ | 85284 | (866) 332-5455 |
| MEDCO CONTAINMENT LIFE INS C | Mechanicsburg | 5010 Ritter Rd Suite 115 | PA | 17055 | (717) 795-9133 |

# South Dakota

## A

| Company | City | Address | State | Zip | Telephone |
|---|---|---|---|---|---|
| MEDICA HEALTH PLANS | Minnetonka | 401 Carlson Parkway | MN | 55305 | (952) 992-2900 |

# South Dakota (continued)

## A-

| Company | City | Address | State | Zip | Telephone |
|---------|------|---------|-------|-----|-----------|
| MEDICA INS CO | Minnetonka | 401 Carlson Parkway | MN | 55305 | (952) 992-2900 |

## B+

| Company | City | Address | State | Zip | Telephone |
|---------|------|---------|-------|-----|-----------|
| COVENTRY HEALTH & LIFE INS CO | Dover | 160 Greentree Dr Suite 101 | DE | 19904 | (800) 843-7421 |
| MEDCO CONTAINMENT LIFE INS C | Mechanicsburg | 5010 Ritter Rd Suite 115 | PA | 17055 | (717) 795-9133 |

# Tennessee

## A+

| Company | City | Address | State | Zip | Telephone |
|---------|------|---------|-------|-----|-----------|
| HEALTH CARE SVC CORP A MUT L | Chicago | 300 East Randolph Street | IL | 60601 | (312) 653-6000 |

## A-

| Company | City | Address | State | Zip | Telephone |
|---------|------|---------|-------|-----|-----------|
| AETNA HEALTH INC (A PA CORP) | Blue Bell | 980 Jolly Rd | PA | 19422 | (800) 872-3862 |
| BLUECROSS BLUESHIELD OF TENN | Chattanooga | 1 Cameron Hill Cir | TN | 37402 | (423) 535-5600 |

## B+

| Company | City | Address | State | Zip | Telephone |
|---------|------|---------|-------|-----|-----------|
| AMERIGROUP TENNESSEE INC | Nashville | 22 Century Blvd Suite 310 | TN | 37214 | (757) 473-2721 |
| COVENTRY HEALTH & LIFE INS CO | Dover | 160 Greentree Dr Suite 101 | DE | 19904 | (800) 843-7421 |
| EXPRESS SCRIPTS INS CO | Tempe | 7909 S Hardy Dr | AZ | 85284 | (866) 332-5455 |
| MEDCO CONTAINMENT LIFE INS C | Mechanicsburg | 5010 Ritter Rd Suite 115 | PA | 17055 | (717) 795-9133 |
| UNITEDHEALTHCARE PLAN RIVER | Moline | 1300 River Drive | IL | 61265 | (309) 736-4600 |

# Texas

## A+

| Company | City | Address | State | Zip | Telephone |
|---------|------|---------|-------|-----|-----------|
| HEALTH CARE SVC CORP A MUT L | Chicago | 300 East Randolph Street | IL | 60601 | (312) 653-6000 |

## A

| Company | City | Address | State | Zip | Telephone |
|---------|------|---------|-------|-----|-----------|
| TEXAS CHILDRENS HEALTH PLAN | Houston | 2450 Holcombe Suite 34L | TX | 77021 | (832) 828-1020 |

## A-

| Company | City | Address | State | Zip | Telephone |
|---------|------|---------|-------|-----|-----------|
| AMERIGROUP TEXAS INC | Grand Prairie | 2505 N Highway 360 Suite 300 | TX | 75050 | (757) 490-6900 |
| COMMUNITY HEALTH CHOICE INC | Houston | 2636 South Loop West Ste 700 | TX | 77054 | (713) 295-2200 |

## B+

| Company | City | Address | State | Zip | Telephone |
|---------|------|---------|-------|-----|-----------|
| COVENTRY HEALTH & LIFE INS CO | Dover | 160 Greentree Dr Suite 101 | DE | 19904 | (800) 843-7421 |
| EXPRESS SCRIPTS INS CO | Tempe | 7909 S Hardy Dr | AZ | 85284 | (866) 332-5455 |
| MEDCO CONTAINMENT LIFE INS C | Mechanicsburg | 5010 Ritter Rd Suite 115 | PA | 17055 | (717) 795-9133 |
| UNITEDHEALTHCARE BENEFITS O | Plano | 5800 Granite Pkwy Suite 900 | TX | 75024 | (972) 866-2693 |
| UNITEDHEALTHCARE COMMUNIT | Houston | 9700 Bissonnet, Ste 2225 | TX | 77036 | (713) 778-8664 |

# Utah

### A+

| Company | City | Address | State | Zip | Telephone |
|---|---|---|---|---|---|
| HEALTH CARE SVC CORP A MUT L | Chicago | 300 East Randolph Street | IL | 60601 | (312) 653-6000 |

### A-

| Company | City | Address | State | Zip | Telephone |
|---|---|---|---|---|---|
| ALTIUS HEALTH PLANS | South Jordan | 10421 S Jordan Gateway Ste 400 | UT | 84095 | (801) 933-3500 |
| HEALTHWISE | Salt Lake City | 2890 E Cottonwood Pkwy | UT | 84121 | (801) 333-2000 |
| SELECTHEALTH INC | Murray | 5381 Green St | UT | 84123 | (801) 442-5000 |

### B+

| Company | City | Address | State | Zip | Telephone |
|---|---|---|---|---|---|
| COVENTRY HEALTH & LIFE INS CO | Dover | 160 Greentree Dr Suite 101 | DE | 19904 | (800) 843-7421 |
| EXPRESS SCRIPTS INS CO | Tempe | 7909 S Hardy Dr | AZ | 85284 | (866) 332-5455 |
| MEDCO CONTAINMENT LIFE INS C | Mechanicsburg | 5010 Ritter Rd Suite 115 | PA | 17055 | (717) 795-9133 |

# Vermont

### A-

| Company | City | Address | State | Zip | Telephone |
|---|---|---|---|---|---|
| BLUE CROSS BLUE SHIELD OF VER | Montpelier | 445 Industrial Ln | VT | 05602 | (802) 223-6131 |

### B+

| Company | City | Address | State | Zip | Telephone |
|---|---|---|---|---|---|
| EXPRESS SCRIPTS INS CO | Tempe | 7909 S Hardy Dr | AZ | 85284 | (866) 332-5455 |
| MEDCO CONTAINMENT LIFE INS C | Mechanicsburg | 5010 Ritter Rd Suite 115 | PA | 17055 | (717) 795-9133 |
| VERMONT HEALTH PLAN LLC | Montpelier | 445 Industrial Ln | VT | 05602 | (802) 223-6131 |

# Virgin Islands of the U.S.

### A-

| Company | City | Address | State | Zip | Telephone |
|---|---|---|---|---|---|
| TRIPLE-S SALUD INC | San Juan | F D Roosevelt Ave 1441 | PR | 00920 | (787) 749-4949 |

# Virginia

### A+

| Company | City | Address | State | Zip | Telephone |
|---|---|---|---|---|---|
| CAREFIRST BLUECHOICE INC | Washington | 840 First Street NE | DC | 20065 | (202) 479-8000 |
| GROUP HOSP & MEDICAL SERVICE | Washington | 840 First Street NE | DC | 20065 | (202) 479-8000 |
| HEALTH CARE SVC CORP A MUT L | Chicago | 300 East Randolph Street | IL | 60601 | (312) 653-6000 |
| HEALTHKEEPERS INC | Richmond | 2015 Staples Mills Road | VA | 23230 | (804) 354-7000 |
| OPTIMA HEALTH PLAN | Virginia Beach | 4417 Corporation Lane | VA | 23462 | (757) 552-7306 |

### A

| Company | City | Address | State | Zip | Telephone |
|---|---|---|---|---|---|
| KAISER PERMANENTE INS CO | Oakland | 300 Lakeside Dr 26th Floor | CA | 94612 | (877) 847-7572 |

### A-

| Company | City | Address | State | Zip | Telephone |
|---|---|---|---|---|---|
| AETNA HEALTH INC (A PA CORP) | Blue Bell | 980 Jolly Rd | PA | 19422 | (800) 872-3862 |

# Virginia (continued)

## B+

| Company | City | Address | State | Zip | Telephone |
|---|---|---|---|---|---|
| COVENTRY HEALTH & LIFE INS CO | Dover | 160 Greentree Dr Suite 101 | DE | 19904 | (800) 843-7421 |
| EXPRESS SCRIPTS INS CO | Tempe | 7909 S Hardy Dr | AZ | 85284 | (866) 332-5455 |
| MEDCO CONTAINMENT LIFE INS C | Mechanicsburg | 5010 Ritter Rd Suite 115 | PA | 17055 | (717) 795-9133 |
| UNITEDHEALTHCARE PLAN RIVER | Moline | 1300 River Drive | IL | 61265 | (309) 736-4600 |

# Washington

## A+

| Company | City | Address | State | Zip | Telephone |
|---|---|---|---|---|---|
| PROVIDENCE HEALTH PLAN | Beaverton | 3601 SW Murray Blvd Ste 10 | OR | 97005 | (503) 574-7500 |

## A-

| Company | City | Address | State | Zip | Telephone |
|---|---|---|---|---|---|
| GROUP HEALTH COOPERATIVE | Seattle | 320 Westlake Ave N Suite 100 | WA | 98109 | (206) 448-5528 |
| KAISER FOUNDATION HP NORTHW | Portland | 500 NE Multnomah St, Suite 100 | OR | 97232 | (503) 813-2800 |
| MOLINA HEALTHCARE OF WASHI | Bothell | 21540 30th Dr SE Ste 400 | WA | 98021 | (425) 424-1100 |
| PREMERA BLUE CROSS | Mountlake Terrac | 7001 220th St SW | WA | 98043 | (425) 918-4000 |

## B+

| Company | City | Address | State | Zip | Telephone |
|---|---|---|---|---|---|
| EXPRESS SCRIPTS INS CO | Tempe | 7909 S Hardy Dr | AZ | 85284 | (866) 332-5455 |
| LIFEWISE HEALTH PLAN OF WASH | Mountlake Terrac | 7001 220th St SW | WA | 98043 | (425) 670-4000 |
| MEDCO CONTAINMENT LIFE INS C | Mechanicsburg | 5010 Ritter Rd Suite 115 | PA | 17055 | (717) 795-9133 |
| REGENCE BL CROSS BL SHIELD OR | Portland | 100 SW Market St | OR | 97201 | (503) 225-5221 |
| REGENCE BLUESHIELD | Seattle | 1800 9th Ave | WA | 98101 | (206) 464-3600 |

# West Virginia

## A+

| Company | City | Address | State | Zip | Telephone |
|---|---|---|---|---|---|
| HEALTH CARE SVC CORP A MUT L | Chicago | 300 East Randolph Street | IL | 60601 | (312) 653-6000 |

## A-

| Company | City | Address | State | Zip | Telephone |
|---|---|---|---|---|---|
| HIGHMARK WEST VIRGINIA INC | Parkersburg | 614 Market St | WV | 26102 | (304) 424-7700 |
| UNICARE HEALTH PLAN OF WEST | Charleston | 707 Virginia St E | WV | 25301 | (877) 864-2273 |

## B+

| Company | City | Address | State | Zip | Telephone |
|---|---|---|---|---|---|
| COVENTRY HEALTH & LIFE INS CO | Dover | 160 Greentree Dr Suite 101 | DE | 19904 | (800) 843-7421 |
| COVENTRY HEALTH CARE OF WES | Charleston | 500 Virginia St E Ste 400 | WV | 25301 | (717) 671-2411 |
| HEALTH PLAN OF THE UPPER OHI | St Clairsville | 52160 National Rd E | OH | 43950 | (740) 695-3585 |
| MEDCO CONTAINMENT LIFE INS C | Mechanicsburg | 5010 Ritter Rd Suite 115 | PA | 17055 | (717) 795-9133 |

# Wisconsin

## A+

| Company | City | Address | State | Zip | Telephone |
|---|---|---|---|---|---|
| HEALTH CARE SVC CORP A MUT L | Chicago | 300 East Randolph Street | IL | 60601 | (312) 653-6000 |
| SECURITY HEALTH PLAN OF WI IN | Marshfield | 1515 Saint Joseph Ave | WI | 54449 | (715) 221-9555 |

# Wisconsin (continued)

## A-

| Company | City | Address | State | Zip | Telephone |
|---|---|---|---|---|---|
| DEAN HEALTH PLAN INC | Madison | 1277 Deming Way | WI | 53717 | (608) 836-1400 |
| HEALTHPARTNERS INS CO | Minneapolis | 8170 33rd Ave S | MN | 55440 | (952) 883-6000 |
| MEDICA INS CO | Minnetonka | 401 Carlson Parkway | MN | 55305 | (952) 992-2900 |

## B+

| Company | City | Address | State | Zip | Telephone |
|---|---|---|---|---|---|
| COMPCARE HEALTH SERVICES INS | Milwaukee | 6775 W Washington St | WI | 53214 | (414) 459-5000 |
| COVENTRY HEALTH & LIFE INS CO | Dover | 160 Greentree Dr Suite 101 | DE | 19904 | (800) 843-7421 |
| EXPRESS SCRIPTS INS CO | Tempe | 7909 S Hardy Dr | AZ | 85284 | (866) 332-5455 |
| MEDCO CONTAINMENT LIFE INS C | Mechanicsburg | 5010 Ritter Rd Suite 115 | PA | 17055 | (717) 795-9133 |
| NETWORK HEALTH INS CORP | Menasha | 1570 Midway Pl | WI | 54952 | (920) 720-1200 |
| NETWORK HEALTH PLAN | Menasha | 1570 Midway Pl | WI | 54952 | (920) 720-1200 |

# Wyoming

## A+

| Company | City | Address | State | Zip | Telephone |
|---|---|---|---|---|---|
| ROCKY MOUNTAIN HEALTH MAIN | Grand Junction | 2775 Crossroads Blvd | CO | 81506 | (970) 244-7760 |

## A-

| Company | City | Address | State | Zip | Telephone |
|---|---|---|---|---|---|
| ALTIUS HEALTH PLANS | South Jordan | 10421 S Jordan Gateway Ste 400 | UT | 84095 | (801) 933-3500 |

## B+

| Company | City | Address | State | Zip | Telephone |
|---|---|---|---|---|---|
| BLUE CROSS BLUE SHIELD OF WY | Cheyenne | 4000 House Ave | WY | 82001 | (307) 634-1393 |
| EXPRESS SCRIPTS INS CO | Tempe | 7909 S Hardy Dr | AZ | 85284 | (866) 332-5455 |
| MEDCO CONTAINMENT LIFE INS C | Mechanicsburg | 5010 Ritter Rd Suite 115 | PA | 17055 | (717) 795-9133 |

# Appendix

# Frequently Asked Questions

**Q: I'm married. Does the HDHP policy have to be in my name to open an HSA?**

**A:** The HDHP policy does not have to be in your name. As long as you have coverage under the HDHP policy, you can be eligible for a HSA assuming you meet the other requirements.

**Q: I understand that my spouse and I can have our own HSAs. But if both of us have family HDHP coverage and one has additional coverage, are both of us eligible for an HSA?**

**A:** Depending on the other coverage, you could both qualify. Imagine you and your spouse have family HDHP coverage with a $3,500 deductible. You have no other coverage. Your spouse also has individual HDHP coverage with a $2,000 deductible. Both of you are eligible individuals and treated as having only family coverage. Even if one of you has a separate family HDHP coverage, as long as the deductible exceeds the minimum, both of you are eligible.

In the event one of you has individual coverage with a lower-than-the-minimum deductible, the one with the low deductible plan is not eligible and cannot contribute to an HSA. Also if one of you is enrolled in Medicare, that individual is not eligible. However, the other spouse can contribute the maximum amount.

**Q: What additional health coverage can I have but still be eligible for an HSA?**

**A:** When you have medical benefits in addition to an HDHP, you have to be careful that it doesn't disqualify you from HSA eligibility.

You can have the following coverage and still be eligible for an HSA:

- Specific disease or illness insurance

- Accident, disability, dental care, vision care, and long-term care insurance

- Auto insurance policies that include health benefits, disability, or long-term care coverage

- Various employer-operated, on-site clinic services that provide free or below-market-rate physicals and immunizations, a variety of nonprescription pain relievers, and treatment for injuries caused by workplace accidents as long as the clinic does not provide significant medical benefits

- Any health insurance plan where the deductible is equal or greater than the statutory minimum HDHP deductible. You could, for example, have a policy that kicked in where your HDHP coverage ended, say at $2 million of lifetime coverage. (It should be noted that effective September 23, 2010 the Patient Protection and Affordable Care Act removed lifetime coverage limits, but annual limits may remain as determined by the Secretary of Health and Human Services.)

**Q: If I sign up for an HSA, can I still use my company's Employee Assistance Program?**

**A:** You may also take part in Employee Assistance Programs, disease management programs, or wellness programs offered by your employer. Preventive care is encouraged and generally does not include any service or benefit intended to treat an existing illness, injury or condition. However, certain drugs and medications can be considered preventive care. An example would be if you have a high cholesterol level and need a cholesterol-lowering drug.

Other preventive care services that an HDHP can provide as first-dollar coverage before the minimum deductible is satisfied include:

- Tobacco cessation programs

- Periodic health evaluations, such as an annual physical

- Screening, such as mammograms

- Immunizations

- Routine pre-natal and well-child care

- Weight loss programs

## Q: What health coverage makes me ineligible for an HSA?

**A:** Generally speaking, health insurance coverage that provides a significant health benefit will make you ineligible for an HSA. More specifically, the following coverage is not acceptable with an HSA:

- Active medical benefits that cover from the first dollar, such as Medicare and Tricare (health coverage for the military). FSAs and HRAs are ineligible too, but with two exceptions: Those with a limited purpose that restrict coverage to certain benefits such as vision, dental, or preventive care; and those that only provide reimbursement after the minimum annual deductible has been satisfied under the HDHP.

---

An important note on Medicare: Once you have enrolled in Medicare, you are no longer eligible for an HSA. But if you are simply eligible for Medicare because you are 65 or have a disability at a younger age and have not actively enrolled in the program, you're still eligible for an HSA if you have a qualifying HDHP.

---

- Your medical expenses covered by your spouse's FSA or HRA before your HDHP deductible is met
- An HDHP that provides a prescription drug benefit with no annual deductible.
- Having an individual deductible within a family HDHP that is below the family deductible required with an HSA

## Q: Can my eligibility status for an HSA change?

**A:** You should keep in mind that if the circumstances of your medical coverage change, your eligibility in an HSA can change too. For example, suppose your employer offers an HRA that reimburses any medical expense you incur. You wouldn't be eligible for an HSA. But if next year your employer amends the coverage to limit its benefits to expenses for vision care, dental care, and preventive care and to pay your share of the premiums for the employer-sponsored HDHP, you would then be eligible for an HSA.

Employers can affect your eligibility in other ways, too. For example what if you have an HDHP and the employer pays or reimburses some or all of your medical expenses incurred before the minimum HDHP deductible is satisfied (other than disregarded coverage or preventive care)? This payment or reimbursement would render you ineligible for an HSA. That's because if at any time, your employer pays or reimburses, directly or indirectly, all or part of your medical expenses below the minimum HDHP deductible, you are not eligible to contribute to an HSA.

**Q: I am a self-employed construction worker, can I have an HSA?**

**A:** Your employment status has no effect on your eligibility. Your eligibility for an HSA is evaluated the same way as an employed person or someone who is not earning a salary. This eligibility test also covers owners and shareholders of S corporations and partners in a partnership or limited liability company.

**Q: Will my HDHP deductible be the same as the HSA deductible??**

**A:** It's important to note that the minimum deductible requirement for an HSA is not necessarily the same as the annual deductible under your HDHP.

For example, suppose during 2013 you had an HDHP with individual coverage and an annual deductible of $4,500. You paid the first $1,500 of covered medical expenses below the deductible, and then your employer reimburses the next $3,000 of covered medical expenses. The $3,000 of medical expenses reimbursed by your employer is not a contribution to an HSA and not disregarded coverage or preventive care. Despite this, because you are responsible for the HSA minimum annual deductible of $1,250 in 2013, you are eligible.

## Q: Can I have a drug discount card?

**A:** Yes you can. Holding a discount card does not affect your eligibility for an HSA.

## Q: As a veteran, am I eligible for an HSA?

**A:** You maintain eligibility for an HSA unless you have actually received VA health benefits in the last three months. This includes receiving treatment at a facility or receiving prescription drug benefits. You would remain eligible if you are eligible for medical benefits through the Department of Veterans Affairs (VA) but only receive medical care that is disregarded coverage or preventive care from the VA and are otherwise eligible.

# IRS Guidance to Includible Medical Expenses

The following list represents illnesses, treatments and other medical expenses allowed under IRS guidelines published in IRS Pub 502 for the 2012 tax year. It is not intended to be an exhaustive listing but does represent a good indication of the expenses that would be approved.

A full explanation of each expense is provided within the IRS publication.

Abortion
Acupuncture
Alcoholism
Ambulance
Annual Physical Examination
Artificial Limb
Artificial teeth
Autoette
Bandages
Birth Control Pills
Body Scan
Braille Books and Magazines
Breast Reconstruction Surgery
Chiropractor
Christian Science Practitioner
Contact Lenses
Crutches
Dental Treatment
Diagnostic Devices
Disabled Dependent Care
Expenses
Drug Addiction
Drugs
Eyeglasses
Eye Surgery
Fertility Enhancement
Guide Dog or Other Service
Animal
Hearing Aids
Home Care
Home Improvements
Hospital Services
Learning Disability
Legal Fees
Lifetime Care – Advance
Payments

Laboratory
Lodging
Lead-Based Paint Removal
Long-Term Care
Meals
Medical Conferences
Medicines
Nursing Home
Nursing Services
Operations
Optometrist
Organ Donors
Osteopath
Oxygen
Physical Examination
Pregnancy Test Kit
Prosthesis
Psychiatric Care
Psychoanalysis
Psychologist
Special Education
Sterilization
Stop Smoking Programs
Surgery
Telephone
Television
Therapy
Transplants
Transportation
Vasectomy
Vision Correction Surgery
Weight-Loss Program
Wheelchair
Wig
X-ray

# Helpful Resources

## Internal Revenue Service Assistance

General tax guidance - www.irs.gov

Medical and dental expense rules for the 2012 tax filing, including guidance on qualified medical expenses can be found in IRS Pub 502 - http://www.irs.gov/pub/irs-pdf/p502.pdf

For prohibited activities see section 4975 of the Internal Revenue Code – http://www.irs.gov/irb/2006-29_IRB/ar06.html

## Treasury Assistance

The US Treasury web site contains:

- All Treasury guidance
- Frequently asked questions
- IRS forms and publications
- HSA statute
- Examples of tax savings from HSA contributions
- Links to other useful sites

http://www.treasury.gov/resource-center/faqs/Taxes/Pages/Health-Savings-Accounts.aspx
For details about Health Savings Accounts in a pdf file try -
http://www.treasury.gov/press-center/press-releases/Documents/hsafab40704.pdf

## What Our Ratings Mean

**A  Excellent.** The company offers excellent financial security. It has maintained a conservative stance in its investment strategies, business operations and underwriting commitments. While the financial position of any company is subject to change, we believe that this company has the resources necessary to deal with severe economic conditions.

**B  Good.** The company offers good financial security and has the resources to deal with a variety of adverse economic conditions. It comfortably exceeds the minimum levels for all of our rating criteria, and is likely to remain healthy for the near future. However, in the event of a severe recession or major financial crisis, we feel that this assessment should be reviewed to make sure that the firm is still maintaining adequate financial strength.

**C  Fair.** The company offers fair financial security and is currently stable. But during an economic downturn or other financial pressures, we feel it may encounter difficulties in maintaining its financial stability.

**D  Weak.** The company currently demonstrates what we consider to be significant weaknesses which could negatively impact policyholders. In an unfavorable economic environment, these weaknesses could be magnified.

**E  Very Weak.** The company currently demonstrates what we consider to be significant weaknesses and has also failed some of the basic tests that we use to identify fiscal stability. Therefore, even in a favorable economic environment, it is our opinion that policyholders could incur significant risks.

**F  Failed.** The company is deemed failed if it is either 1) under supervision of an insurance regulatory authority; 2) in the process of rehabilitation; 3) in the process of liquidation; or 4) voluntarily dissolved after disciplinary or other regulatory action by an insurance regulatory authority.

**+  The plus sign** is an indication that the company is at the upper end of the letter grade rating.

**-  The minus sign** is an indication that the company is at the lower end of the letter grade rating.

**U  Unrated Companies.** The company is unrated for one or more of the following reasons: 1) total assets are less than $1 million; 2) premium income for the current year is less than $100,000; 3) the company functions almost exclusively as a holding company rather than as an underwriter; or 4) we do not have enough information to reliably issue a rating.